The Wagon Box Fight

An Episode of Red Cloud's War

Jerry Keenan

With a Summary of Historical Archaeology
at the Wagon Box Site

Savas Publishing Company

The Wagon Box Fight:: An Episode of Red Cloud's War
by Jerry Keenan

© 2000 Jerry Keenan

Includes bibliographic references and index

Printing Number
10 9 8 7 6 5 4 3 2 1

ISBN 1-882810-87-2

Savas Publishing Company
476 West Elm Street, P.O. Box 307
Conshohocken, PA 19428

(800) 418-6065 (distribution)

The "Wagon Box Fight" originally appeared in the January 1972 issue of *Journal of the West*. A selection of articles from that issue, including "The Wagon Box Fight," was also published in book form in 1972 by Pruett Publishing Company under the title *Hostiles and Horse Soldiers*, Lonnie J. White, ed.
    The first Fort Phil Kearny / Bozeman Trail Association edition of *The Wagon Box Fight* was published in 1988, and a revised edition was issued in 1990. The Lightning Tree edition was published in 1992.

This book is printed on 50-lb. acid-free paper. It meets or exceeds the guidelines for permanence and durability of the Committee on Production Guidelines for Book Longevity of the Council on Library Resources

To the late. . .

J. W. Vaughn
Elsa Spear
Ed Smyth
Carl Oslund

Table of Contents

List of Photos & Illustrations

Maps

Archaeological Survey Figures

Preface

In the preface to the previous edition of this work, I suggested that the study of history was an evolutionary process, one that is continually undergoing refinement. The publication of this, the fourth edition of *The Wagon Box Fight*, further reinforces that belief.

Three reasons motivated me to undertake a new edition. First, since the publication of the third edition (1990), the discovery of additional details regarding the fight suggested that the story would be clarified and enhanced by the incorporation of this new information. Second, the 1997 issuance, by the state of Wyoming, of the results of its archaeological survey of the wagon box area, provided another sound reason for preparing a new edition. Although none of the above altered, in a significant way, the fundamental conclusions reached in earlier editions of this work, their inclusion here provides a more complete understanding of the event and its aftermath. Finally, expanding the study to present an overview of the Bozeman Trail, Red Cloud's War, and Fort Phil Kearny, put the central story of the Wagon Box Fight in a stronger and more meaningful historical perspective.

The preparation of a new edition also holds a certain attraction because it offers the author an opportunity to modify viewpoints and address minor corrections, which somehow always seem to be necessary in any new edition no matter how many times it has been revised. An author can always find something in need of "bettering." In all, it is hoped that with this new and expanded version, the reader will gain a better understanding of the Wagon Box Fight's role in the larger context of those tumultuous days of which it was a part.

I extend my appreciation once again to those that offered help and encouragement, provided research materials, or in some way made a contribution to the previous edition. In particular, I would like to thank Mary Ellen McWilliams, H. Sterling Fenn, John D. McDermott, the late Carl Oslund, Susan Badger Doyle, Fr. Barry Hagan, Alan Bourne, the late Ed Smyth, Margie Claus Duppong, Douglas C. McChristian, Sonny Reisch, Bob Wilson, the late Bob Murray, Mike Koury and Glen Perkins.

For help and assistance in preparing this fourth edition, I wish to express my appreciation to Arlene Ekland-Earnst, Curator of the Wyoming Pioneer Museum, Douglas, Wyoming, Helen Graham of the Sheridan County Fulmer Public Library, and Joseph Marshall. A special thanks to Mark Miller and Danny Walker of the Wyoming State Archaeologist's office, and Jeff Hauff, formerly of the Wyoming Division of State Parks and Historic Sites for preparing the summary of their archaeological field work for use in this edition.

As always, my wife, Carol has been a reservoir of encouragement and support for which an expression of appreciation seems entirely inadequate.

To any I may have inadvertently overlooked, my apologies and to all who in any way made a contribution to this effort, my sincere appreciation. For any errors that have somehow managed to survive, I bear full responsibility.

Special thanks are due the Fort Phil Kearny/Bozeman Trail Association for continued support.

Jerry Keenan

Longmont, Colorado

Chapter 1

The Bozeman Trail

T he discovery of gold in southwestern Montana late in 1862 produced an almost overnight rush to the promised riches of Alder Gulch, Bannack, and Virginia City. Travelers from the west reached the gold camps from Fort Hall, Idaho, or via the Mullen Road that ran from Fort Walla Walla, Washington Territory to Fort Benton, Montana. Prior to the creation of the Bozeman Trail, those wishing to reach the area from the East traveled by steamer up the Missouri River to Fort Benton, then overland to the gold camps. Another option was to follow the old Oregon-California Trail west to either Fort Bridger in southwest Wyoming, or Salt Lake City, then north via Fort Hall (present Pocatello, Idaho) and on to the gold fields. The river route, however, was more expensive and of course only open to travel when the river was free of ice. The Oregon Trail-Fort Hall route was circuitous and also time consuming. Thus, necessity soon created the need for a shorter overland route from the states.[1]

In 1863, John Bozeman and a partner, John Jacobs, pioneered a new route that split off from the Oregon-California Trail at three different locations along the North Platte River beyond Fort Laramie. The new route ran north along the eastern apron of the Big Horn Mountains into Montana, where it swung west and continued on to the gold fields, in places paralleling much of today's Interstate Highways 25 and 90. The Bozeman Trail[2] as it would eventually come to be known, was more direct and hence shorter for travelers than going by way of Fort Hall. The chief drawback to the Bozeman Trail was that its course lay through the heart of the Powder River hunting grounds of the Lakota Sioux. Thus, while shorter, it was also considerably more dangerous.[3]

Yet another route to the gold camps was one laid out by famed mountain man Jim Bridger, The so-called Bridger cut-off moved north along the west side of the Big Horn Mountains. The advantage of Bridger's route seems to have been that it was comparatively free from the danger of Indian attack. Although water and forage were not really plentiful on either route, both were apparently scarcer along Bridger's trail. Accordingly, given the somewhat shorter overall distance, together with the promise of slightly better water and forage en route, Bozeman's route eventually became the preferred choice of overland travelers bound for the gold camps, despite the omni-present danger of Indian attack.[4]

Red Cloud's War

Due to Indian troubles, the Bozeman Trail was officially closed in 1865, but emigrant traffic resumed the following year. In order to provide a secure corridor of travel, the U.S. government decided to establish a series

of military outposts at strategic points along the trail. To carry out this assignment, the army selected the Eighteenth U.S. Infantry, commanded by Colonel Henry Beebe Carrington.[5]

An intellectual and an academic, Carrington was an 1845 graduate of Yale law school. Moving to Ohio in 1848, he entered law practice and was later

Col. Henry B. Carrington

*American Heritage Center,
University of WY*

appointed adjutant general of that state by his former partner who was elected governor in 1860. With the outbreak of the Civil War in 1861, Carrington, a devout abolitionist and staunch Union man, was named colonel of the Eighteenth U.S. Infantry. The appointment was entirely political, a reward for his republican zeal. Although his regiment would see much action during the Civil War, Carrington would not be the one to lead it in battle. Instead, he remained behind, serving as assistant to the governor of Indiana, in which capacity he apparently spent most of his time on witch hunts, trying to ferret out those disloyal to the Union. Consequently, while most of the officers in his regiment had seen plenty of combat by the war's end, Carrington had seen none and, in fact, had no actual field experience whatever.

Henry B. Carrington may have lacked experience in battle, but he was not at all bereft of ability. He was a brilliant scholar. He took his colonelcy seriously and studied voraciously, amassing a great store of information about military science, tactics, engineering, and artillery. Unfortunately, he never had an opportunity to field test any of his book learning prior to being given the Bozeman Trail assignment, although as subsequent events were to demonstrate, his lack of leadership as a field commander suggests this would probably have been academic anyway. Thus, notwithstanding his dedication and intellectual prowess, Carrington must be viewed as a poor choice for the Bozeman Trail command.[6]

Poor choice or not he embraced the assignment with zeal and eagerness, and on May 19, 1866, marched out of Fort Kearny[7] near present Kearney, Nebraska, leading two battalions of the Eighteenth Infantry. Carrington's command numbered approximately 700 officers and men of varied experience; some were raw recruits, while others were Civil War veterans. Horses were obtained for about 200 men, thereby providing the expedition with a modest cavalry force. Supplies, equipment, family possessions, and a wide variety of tools, including two sawmills, were hauled in some 226 wagons. The expedition also included a number of women and children, among whom were Carrington's wife, Margaret, and their two sons. The celebrated frontiersman, Jim Bridger, and another veteran of the plains, one H. Williams, had hired on as expedition guides.[8]

On June 13, the column reached Fort Laramie where U.S. government officials were then in the process of conducting treaty negotiations with representatives of the Lakota Sioux nation. The government's primary objective was to make arrangements for white emigrant travel over the Bozeman Trail and the erection of military outposts along it. Apparently the point about army presence along the trail was glossed over by the peace commissioners, because the Indians seem not to have had a clear understanding of what was afoot.

Carrington's arrival, however, suddenly brought everything into sharp focus. Whatever interest there might have been in effecting an amicable agreement promptly dissolved; what had been a fragile trust to begin with was now shattered. The powerful and influential Oglala leaders, Red Cloud and Old-Man-Afraid-Of-His-Horses, angrily severed negotiations when they noted Carrington's arrival. Incensed at what they regarded as the white man's duplicity, they withdrew from the conference, warning that travel through the land of the Lakota would not be permitted. Accordingly, the council was a bust, for without the participation of the Powder River Sioux no agreement was worth the paper on which it was written.[9]

Undeterred, Carrington continued his northward march from Fort Laramie on June 17, reaching the site of Fort Reno (formerly Fort Connor) east of present day Kaycee, Wyoming, on June 28. General Patrick Connor had established a post here the previous year, during the course of his Powder River campaign.

Carrington's instructions called for him to relieve the two companies of Civil War volunteers stationed there and to then move on and establish a

Red Cloud
Smithsonian Institution

new post farther north. However, finding a much more substantial stock of supplies than he had anticipated, Carrington made the decision to retain the present site of Fort Reno (its name had officially been changed to Fort Reno the previous November) as the first of three outposts along the Bozeman Trail. Carrington designated one company of the Eighteenth Infantry as the new Fort Reno garrison, relieving the volunteers. However, following the receipt of new orders from department headquarters in Omaha, a second company soon doubled the garrison's strength.[10] Having thus attended to the establishment of his first outpost, Carrington resumed his northward journey. In the distance could be seen the glorious snow-capped peaks of the mighty Big Horns, undoubtedly a welcome vision to the hot and weary travelers.

Fort Phil Kearny: Hated Post on the Piney

Near noon on Friday, July 13, the Carrington cavalcade reached Piney Creek. In retrospect, at least, the day itself would seem to have been an ominous portent, though the sheer beauty of the surrounding landscape surely would have made it difficult to imagine the tragedies and travails that were to unfold here in the months ahead.

During the next twenty-four hours, Carrington, in company with several officers, a mounted detachment, and guide Jim Bridger, explored the surrounding area in search of the right site for another post. This second outpost would serve as his flagship station—the headquarters post for the newly created Mountain District, Department of the Platte. His survey completed, Carrington selected a bench of land between the forks of the Piney Creeks. Here, on July 15, ground was broken and construction began on a new post to be named Fort Phil Kearny.

Work progressed rapidly that summer and by early autumn Carrington's soldiers had completed a 600 x 800-foot stockade, together with several buildings. Work on additional structures continued throughout the fall and winter as weather permitted. Unlike Eastern forts of the colonial period, which were frequently subjected to direct attack, most western military posts seldom had to contend with that danger and so did not often enclose a fort inside a stockade. Carrington, however, apparently believed it was necessary in this instance and certainly as one historian has pointed out, the presence of a stockade must have given the garrison an increased sense of security. But not everyone agreed. On a departmental inspection trip in August, Colonel William B. Hazen

Fort Phil Kearny Area Map

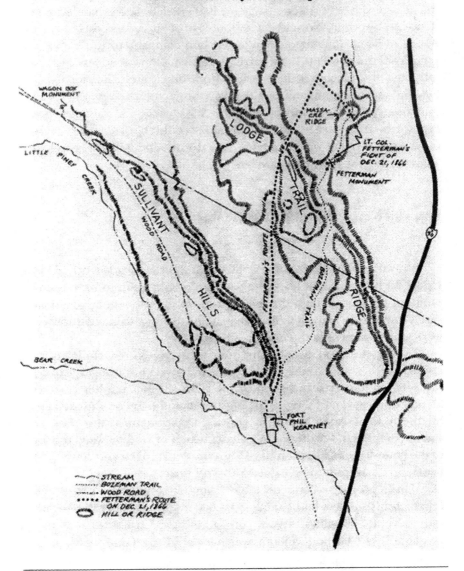

complimented Carrington on the design and construction of the new post, but was nevertheless critical of the stockade feature, believing it unnecessary given the size of the garrison.[11]

To construct a post the size of Fort Phil Kearny required a great deal of lumber. Fortunately, a plentiful supply of timber was available on what was called "Piney Island," or "Piney Flats," a large forested area some five miles northwest of the fort.[12] This area featured a heavy growth of excellent trees, with many running "ninety feet to the first limb, and as straight as an arrow." Early maps showed the area as being enclosed by North and South Piney Creeks, thus presenting an island-like configuration, hence the name Piney Island. On a daily basis, wood cutting details plied the course between Piney Island and the sawmill that was set up near the fort, hauling freshly cut timber for the mill's voracious appetite.[13]

Carrington himself seems to have been personally involved in virtually every aspect of Fort Phil Kearny's construction. This may be attributed partly to his own intense dedication to the project, and partly to an inability to delegate responsibility to his subordinates. In fairness to Carrington, though, it has been pointed out that his officers demonstrated a rather lackluster attitude toward their assignment. Still, a more forceful commander might have gotten more out of his staff. The problem may have been one of resentment at having to serve under Carrington, a desk officer. Whatever the reason, Carrington's solution seems to have been to assume a more prominent personal role than might otherwise have been the case with a different commander. In any event, the situation illustrated, early on, the bad chemistry that existed between Carrington and his staff.[14]

Carrington has also been criticized, and probably justly so, for concentrating on the fort and ignoring the military fitness of his command. Indeed, construction of the post seemed very nearly a passion with him. One can sympathize with his sense of urgency about finishing the job before winter set in, but perhaps some time might have been devoted to training, particularly since most of the garrison was composed of recruits who were still learning the basic skills of soldiering.[15]

Early in August, Carrington dispatched two additional companies under Captain Nathaniel Kinney to construct yet another fort. Located near the Big Horn River, some ninety miles northwest of Fort Phil Kearny, Fort C. F. Smith would be the third Bozeman Trail outpost. The detachment of Kinney's command reduced Fort Phil Kearny's garrison strength to some 300 officers and men.[16]

Ft. Phil Kearny as
drawn by Antonio Nicoli,
2d Cavalry Bugler

National Archives

From the outset it was clear that Indian reaction to the army's presence in the Powder River country was one of strong resentment, particularly among the Lakota. Although all three Bozeman Trail outposts were subjected to harassment by Indian war parties, Fort Phil Kearny was accorded far more attention than either of its sister posts. The fort itself, known to the Indians as the "hated post on the Piney," was never in any real danger, however, and, oddly, neither did the Indians seem to really bother the small community of civilian cabins and shacks that sprang into existence beyond the pale of the stockade.[17]

Nevertheless, the danger of molestation by Indians was very real. War parties lurked in the surrounding hills, ready to dash in and run off grazing livestock, or swoop down on some unsuspecting soul careless enough to stray too far from the post.[18] Livestock, especially horses, was an irresistible attraction. The horse was an essential part of their culture and all of the buffalo-hunting plains tribes excelled at horse thievery; it was a way of life with them.

Another particularly tempting target for Indian raiders was the slow-moving wood train as it lumbered back and forth between the "pineries" and the sawmill. Very often the sentry on Pilot Knob, a high point immediately south of the fort would spot a wood train under attack and signal the alarm. The typical response was for a detachment of soldiers, sometimes accompanied by civilians, to ride out in relief of the besieged train. Seldom, however, were they successful in chastising the Indians. It was frustrating duty.[19]

Wood trains followed a course along the western flank of a land mass known as Sullivant Hills.[20] This route—known appropriately enough as the wood road— roughly parallels that of the present county road leading to the community of Story, but followed a course higher up on the slope of Sullivant Hills. This course meant a tougher pull, especially for the loaded wood trains, but the openness of the land here, compared to the brushy nature of the terrain lower down along the route of the present county road, would also have made it more difficult for the Indian war parties to ambush the wood train. There is reason to believe that the wood road may actually have consisted of two roads, separated by an interval of fifty to one hundred yards. Trains were sent out from the fort in pairs. In the event of Indian attack, they provided support for each other by forming a defensive square according to a pre-arranged plan.[21] Upon reaching the general vicinity of the timber cutting operation, the wood road forked. One segment branched off to the lower pinery, while the other continued on to the upper pinery, located in Piney Flats, about one-quarter to one-half a

The possible remains of what may have been a blockhouse used in defense of the side camp. The large wagon box monument may be seen in the extreme left center. *Ed Smyth*

mile beyond the site of the present rock monument commemorating the wagon box fight.[22]

Although the army was expected to provide protection against Indian attacks, the contractor's working parties were always well armed and ready to take an active role in their own defense. Loggers, livestock herders, and hay-cutters all supplemented whatever protection the army provided. In addition, the civilian contractor constructed three small defensive blockhouses at the pineries, though the size of these structures and whether they were large enough to accommodate the entire working party is unknown. Neither is it known how effective a deterrent they were against Indian attacks.[23]

In November, the arrival of 45 infantrymen, together with 60 men of Company C, Second Cavalry, raised Carrington's total strength to 400 officers and men. The cavalrymen, however, were poorly armed and most of them could scarcely ride. So, overall, the addition of these troops was of questionable value.[24]

The weapons of Carrington's command were a mixed lot. Most of the infantry were armed with the Civil War-vintage Springfield muzzle-loaders. Some of the cavalry also carried Springfields, along with a few Starr breech-loading carbines. In addition to their shoulder arms, the cavalrymen carried either a Colt or Remington revolver. Oddly, the regimental band was armed with the much more effective Spencer breech-loading carbine, which Carrington wisely soon exchanged for the cavalry's Springfields. Officers were free to carry a weapon of their choice.[25]

The Fetterman Disaster

Arriving in November, along with the reinforcements, was a man destined to play a key role in the Fort Phil Kearny saga: Captain (and Brevet Lieutenant Colonel) William Judd Fetterman. A member of the Eighteenth Infantry and a hardened combat veteran of the Civil War, Fetterman was aggressive and brave, perhaps to a fault. He quickly found himself at odds with Carrington's policy regarding Indians, and his views did not lack for support. But there was more to it than that. Carrington's leadership left much to be desired. In addition to his lack of combat experience, Carrington, by nature a thoughtful and usually gentle man, was a poor disciplinarian, so that it is not surprising that his subordinates found the command situation at Fort Phil Kearny increasingly intolerable.

Fetterman and several other officers, including Captain Fred Brown and Lieutenants George Grummond and William Bisbee, formed a core of opposition that managed to undermine Carrington's authority. It is tempting, and not altogether unreasonable, to argue that a more effective field commander simply would not have tolerated what at times amounted to insubordination. Carrington was in a difficult situation. He had few supporters and his options in dealing with these dissident voices were limited. As long as they obeyed orders, albeit even while murmuring, there was little he could do. Certainly there was no way of replacing these officers, though he may well have wished that this might happen. For the time being, anyway, they were stuck with each other.[26]

The crux of their contempt for Carrington centered around a conviction that his defensive strategy regarding

Capt. William J. Fetterman

National Archives

Indians was absolutely the wrong tact. The Indians needed to be chastised, and soundly! Carrington, on the other hand had come into the Powder River country under orders to provide protection for immigrant travelers along the Bozeman Trail; that was his mission. While his orders provided ample latitude to retaliate when attacked, it was not the government's intent that he conduct offensive operations, and moreover he lacked the resources to do so anyway. Nevertheless, Fetterman and the others felt that Carrington's approach was too soft.[27]

The picture changed somewhat in November when General Philip St. George Cooke, commanding the Department of the Platte, issued a directive from his Omaha office authorizing Carrington to launch a strike against the Indians in their winter camps. The directive, prompted as a result of continuing Indian raids and harassment, was no doubt greeted enthusiastically by those who opposed Carrington's passive tactics.[28]

At any rate, less than a month later Carrington was afforded an opportunity to act on Cooke's directive. On December 6, lookouts reported that the wood train was under attack. In response, Carrington sent Captain Fetterman and Lieutenant Horatio Bingham with 30 men to relieve the train. Meanwhile, Carrington and Lieutenant George Grummond, with 25 mounted infantry, proposed to swing around and hit the Indian raiders—believed to be about 100 in number—from behind.[29]

On the face of it the plan sounded good, but things went awry quickly. Fetterman's inexperienced troopers broke when the Indians came at them. In the melee, Lieutenant Bingham was cut off from his men and killed, and the plan simply unraveled from there. Instead of catching the raiders between them, as originally planned, Carrington and Fetterman wound up in separate fights and were fortunate to escape with their respective commands intact. It was to prove a harbinger of disaster.

Thirteen days later, on December 19, the Indians again struck the wood train. The wagons were relieved by a column under the command of Captain (and Brevet Major) James Powell, who wisely declined to pursue the attackers. Forty-eight hours later, on the twenty-first, the wood train was once more under attack and Carrington again ordered Powell to relieve the train. Fetterman, however, probably still smarting from the episode of December 6, requested the assignment on the basis of his seniority (he was a brevet lieutenant colonel and thereby outranked Powell.) Carrington acquiesced, undoubtedly feeling bound to honor the army's command system. Privately, he would have much preferred to send Powell, whom he knew would exercise restraint and good judgement.[30]

In any event, Fetterman was ordered to *only* relieve the wood train. Under no circumstances was he to pursue the raiders over the large land mass known as Lodge Trail Ridge to the east of the fort. Fetterman's command was composed of 49 infantry, and 27 cavalrymen under Lieutenant Grummond. Captain Fred Brown, who was shortly due to return to the states, joined Fetterman, reportedly for one last chance to bring back Red Cloud's scalp. In addition, two civilians, Issac Fisher and James Wheatley, both armed with sixteen-shot Henry repeating rifles, also attached themselves to the column.[31] In all, Fetterman's command numbered three officers, 76 enlisted men, and two civilians, a total of 81. Much has been made of this number having a prophetic ring, since Fetterman had earlier boasted that with a company of soldiers—sixty to a hundred—he could ride through the whole Sioux nation. After the fight, the boast soon became 80 men, rather than a company.[32]

Fetterman, of course, did cross over Lodge Trail Ridge. Unfortunately, little is known of what happened to him and his men after the command disappeared beyond that hulking prominence. Like Custer a decade later, speculation and theories abound, but all that is known for certain is that there were no survivors from Fetterman's command. The available evidence suggests that Fetterman may have been drawn into an elaborately conceived trap by a decoy party that perhaps included a rising young warrior named Crazy Horse. Indeed, one historian has called it the "deadliest trap ever laid by Indians on the northern plains."[33] In any case, Fetterman's command was overwhelmed and destroyed. Fetterman, Brown and a handful of others made their last stand at the site of the large stone obelisk rising above U.S. Highway 87.[34]

The destruction of Fetterman and his entire command was a shocking defeat for the United States Army, though certainly not the first such disaster in its history. The ignominious defeats inflicted on Generals Harmar and St. Clair in the old Northwest Territory had been far worse, but that had been three-quarters of a century earlier and those memories had dimmed as the nation pushed westward. Nothing like this had occurred since the country first began spreading across the Mississippi River in force. Thus, the Fetterman disaster[*] represented the worst such

---

[*] This engagement is sometimes incorrectly call the Fetterman "Massacre." It was a "fight" or "battle," and certainly a disaster, but definitely not a "massacre," which, by definition implies the indiscriminate slaughter of helpless human beings or animals. Fetterman's command, though overwhelmed by numbers, was hardly helpless. It is, as well, incorrect to state or imply that this was a fight with no survivors, unless one is referring strictly to the army, because the vast majority of the Indians involved were clearly survivors.

Marker commemorating the Fetterman Fight, December 21, 1866. *Author*

setback the army had suffered on the Western frontier up to that time, and would remain so until the debacle on the Little Bighorn a decade later.

Conversely, the battle of the "Hundred in the Hands," or the "Fight of the One Hundred," as it was known to the Indians, was a great victory for the Lakota and their allies. Their triumph over Fetterman proved to be the capstone of Red Cloud's two-year struggle to expunge the military from the Powder River country.[35]

Aftermath

In the immediate aftermath of the stunning disaster, a savage blizzard howled across the land of the Pineys. Snow piled high against the stockade, fueling a fear that the Indians would attempt to follow up their victory over Fetterman with an attack on the fort itself, a dread that proved groundless. Carrington was shaken to the core, as well he might have been, and quickly prepared a dispatch to department headquarters requesting reinforcements for his beleaguered command.

The dispatch was given to a pair of civilian couriers, John "Portugee" Phillips and David Dixon, who were hired to take Carrington's message to the nearest telegraph station at Horseshoe Creek, some 200 miles to the south. At Fort Reno, Phillips was asked by Colonel (and Brevet Brigadier General) Henry W. Wessells to continue on to Fort Laramie after stopping at Horseshoe Station, and deliver a message to Colonel Innis Palmer, commanding at Fort Laramie.

At Reno, three other men joined Phillips and Dixon and the five then headed on to Horseshoe Creek, which place they reached at mid-morning on Christmas day. From here, Carrington's shocking dispatch detailing the slaughter of Fetterman and his men was sent to Platte Department headquarters in Omaha. Phillips, after a brief rest, continued on to Fort Laramie, where he arrived late that night.[36]

In response to Carrington's request, General Cooke immediately dispatched reinforcements from Fort Laramie and also ordered a change in command. Accordingly, on January 18, 1867, three companies of

infantry and two of cavalry under Colonel Wessells arrived at Fort Phil Kearny, ending a crisis that was largely imaginary, though certainly understandable.[37] Upon his arrival, Wessells promptly assumed command of the fort and its jittery

Gen. Henry W. Wessells

American Heritage Center,
University of WY

garrison, relieving of Carrington of duty. Five days later, at 1:00 p.m. on January 23, Carrington, his family, and the new widow, Francis Grummond, in company with a mixed escort of cavalry and infantry, left Fort Phil Kearny en route to Fort Caspar, newly designated headquarters post of the Eighteenth Infantry.[38]

Carrington had actually requested this transfer back on July 30. Forty-eight hours earlier, on July 28, Congress had enacted legislation authorizing a reorganization of the U.S. Army. As a result, all three-battalion regiments—including Carrington's Eighteenth Infantry—reverted to single battalion size. The change allowed the second and third battalions of these units to be reconstituted as new regiments. Thus, the second and third battalions of the Eighteenth were redesignated the Twenty-seventh and Thirty-sixth Infantry regiments, respectively, and the first battalion alone would now stand as the Eighteenth Infantry.[39]

Carrington, apparently wishing to remain with the Eighteenth, had requested reassignment as colonel of the first battalion, in effect still commander of the Eighteenth Infantry. His request had been approved, though it was not until December 21—the very day that Fetterman's command was being destroyed—that orders were actually cut reassigning staff and headquarters, Eighteenth Infantry, to Fort Caspar.

Five days later, on December 26, Carrington, too, was reassigned. Unfortunately for him, the timing was terrible. To the public, the media, and to many within the army itself, it appeared that the reassignment stood as censure for the Fetterman disaster. Carrington, of course, was quick to point out that the transfer had been in the works for some time and it was only coincidental that it happened in the wake of the Fetterman debacle. But the colonel was swimming upstream against public opinion. This, after all, was an event of some magnitude. Someone was going to have to be held accountable and with Fetterman dead, the next logical choice was Carrington himself, or so the reasoning went in many quarters. Carrington's departure from Fort Kearny was seen as *prima facie* evidence that the army held Carrington responsible for the tragedy, even though a court of inquiry later exonerated the colonel of any culpability.

At any rate, when the Carrington party headed south in the snow and bitter cold of that January afternoon, the first chapter of the Fort Phil Kearny story had been written.[40]

Chapter 2

The Wagon Box Fight

On August 2, 1867, the army exacted a measure of retribution for the Fetterman disaster of December 21, 1866. The encounter, known as the Wagon Box Fight, was a clash of arms that took place just three miles from where Fetterman's command had been annihilated eight months earlier. Though it was strictly a tactical victory and had no lasting effect on the status of the military in the Powder River country, the Wagon Box Fight continues to attract the attention of writers and students of the Indian wars.

High drama, controversy, and mystery are key ingredients in the popularity of any historical event. Without a generous dose of at least one of these elements, an event is unlikely to hold much popular appeal, though it need have none of the three to possess historical significance. Thus, the Northwest Ordinance of 1787, one of the most significant acts of U.S. history, holds little attraction for any but serious scholars, while the story of the Little Bighorn is well known to the American public. The Wagon Box Fight, while lacking the intensity of attention that has been focused on Custer, nevertheless possesses each of the three characteristics mentioned above in sufficient quantity to continue to attract attention.[41]

Some have seen the Wagon Box Fight as a defining moment of the Indian wars. Clarence Reckmeyer of the Nebraska State Historical Society, for instance, thought it the "greatest of all western Indian battles, not excepting the Custer massacre." It probably should not be surprising that such a view took root. Early accounts of the battle, often shaped by the power of the author's imagination, and fueled by the recollections of aging survivors, created a perception of the fight that was out of all proportion to its true historical significance. Participant Max Littman, for example, claimed that "No such battle as this has ever been recorded in all the Indian engagements of the west. . . . [I]t was the greatest Indian battle of the world." And Littman's comrade in arms, Sam Gibson, who went on to serve forty-eight years in the army, later said his nerves were never again ". . .put to the test they sustained on that terrible 2d of August, 1867, when we fought Red Cloud's warriors in the wagon box corral." Thus, the fight obviously came to be thought of by many as a confrontation of epic proportions.[42]

The arrival of the Wessells relief column increased the overall strength of Fort Phil Kearny by nearly 300 men and surely did much to allay the concerns of a nervous garrison. But as the winter continued to unfold it turned out that there was less to fear from the Indians than had been expected. Dwindling supplies of food and forage proved a far more serious

Col. Jonathan E. Smith

Wyoming Division of Cultural Resources

threat. The reinforcements, while providing Fort Kearny with more muscle, also placed a severe drain on the fort's supply system, creating a shortage of food and animal forage that was not alleviated until spring and the arrival of the first bull trains from Fort Laramie.[43]

Warmer weather, however, also heralded a renewal of the Indians' harassment of the Bozeman Trail and the three forts created to provide protection along its course, especially Fort Phil Kearny. Notwithstanding, on July 3, 1867, J. R. Porter, a civilian contractor representing the firm of Proctor and Gilmore, arrived at Fort Phil Kearny with a welcome supply train. Accompanying the train was Fort Phil Kearny's new commanding officer, Colonel John Eugene Smith, Twenty-seventh Infantry, a first rate leader and an officer with a splendid record.[44]

In addition to food and other supplies, Porter's train carried a shipment of seven hundred Springfield-Allin breech-loading rifles and 100,000 rounds of .50-70-450 Martin bar-anvil, center-fire primed cartridges. Long overdue, these new weapons represented a dramatic improvement over the old .58 caliber Civil War muzzle-loaders with which the infantry at Fort Phil Kearny, including those under Fetterman's command, had been equipped. Issuance of the new weapons took place soon after the arrival of Porter's bull train.[45]

The new breech-loader fired a bullet approximately 1/2-inch in diameter. The bullet was propelled by 70 grains of black powder and weighed 450 grains (slightly less than an ounce). Hence, the numerical description .50-70-450. Manufactured at the Frankford, Philadelphia Arsenal, the cartridges were packed in 20-round paper boxes, 50 boxes per case. Although the army had

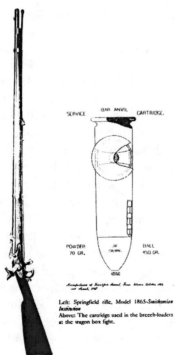

Left: Springfield rifle, Model 1865-*Smithsonian Institution*
Above: The cartridge used in the breech-loaders at the wagon box fight.

Far left: Springfield Rifle, Model 1865. *Smithsonian Institution.*

Left: The cartridge used in the breech-loader at the wagon box fight.

used a variety of breech-loading rifles and carbines during the Civil War with considerable success, the .58 caliber Springfield muzzle- loader remained the primary infantry weapon at the war's end in 1865.[46]

Faced with the reality that the breech-loader was a weapon whose time had arrived, the army sought a way to achieve a practical and economical transition to this system. The problem was that after four years of war, there was no money to spend on new weapons. The solution: recycle the large, leftover inventory of Civil War muzzle-loaders. Accordingly, in 1865, Erskine S. Allin of the National Armory in Springfield, Massachusetts, was authorized to develop a method of converting muzzle-loaders to breech-loaders. Allin's efforts resulted in the development of a single-shot, breech-loading system that he patented in September 1865. The design was approved by the War Department, which subsequently authorized the armory to convert a number of muzzle-loaders to the .58-caliber rimfire Allin conversion, M-1865 Springfield rifle.[47]

However, in March 1866, a military board decided that the standard infantry rifle should be reduced from .58 to .50-caliber. This modification required the newly converted breech-loaders to have their bores reamed to accept .50-caliber liners that were then brazed into place. It was this modified version, known as the *second* Allin conversion, M-1866, Springfield rifle, .50-caliber center-fire that arrived at Fort Phil Kearny on Porter's bull train.[48]

Fort Phil Kearny observed July 4th, Independence Day, by firing a salute of 38 guns at meridian (noon) and "work was suspended for the day." On July 5, Colonel Smith officially assumed command of the post, replacing Colonel Wessells. Coincidentally, Colonel Smith's new second-in-command was Major Benjamin Smith, who had also arrived with Porter's bull train. The two men were unrelated, but both had distinguished Civil War records, John Smith having been breveted major general of volunteers, and Benjamin, brigadier general of volunteers.[49]

Throughout the month of July 1867, Lakota war parties continually harassed the hay-cutters and the wood train, and made repeated attempts to drive off the animal herds grazing in the immediate vicinity of Fort Phil Kearny. In the main, however, these seem to have been low key efforts and while always threatening, were an annoyance more than anything.[50]

Providing protection for the woodcutting operation posed a difficult challenge because of the distance separating the cutting area from the fort. The "upper pinery" was located near the South Fork Canyon of South or Big Piney Creek, north of the large rock marker at the site of the wagon box corral, while the "lower pinery" was situated near the mouth of Little

Piney Creek Canyon, southwest of the rock marker. Both sites served as bases for smaller "side camps."[51]

Upon his arrival at Fort Phil Kearny, Porter was awarded a contract by the post quartermaster, Captain George Dandy, to supply the fort with timber and fuel. The contract stipulated that the quartermaster would provide wagons, while the contractor supplied the necessary complement of woodcutters and livestock herders. It was also understood that the army would furnish guard and escort details for the operation.[52]

Early in July, the contractors erected a corral of wagon boxes on an open plain near the pineries. This corral served as the field headquarters and central collection area for the wood cutting operation. Freshly cut timber was brought to the corral from the "pineries," from where it was then hauled to the fort. The "running gear" or chassis of the wagons, was used to transport the cut timber, an arrangement that left the tops, or "boxes," or "beds" of the wagons available for use as a corral. The corral itself served a two-fold purpose: first, it provided a secure area where livestock would be safe from night raids by the Indians. Secondly, it stood as a defensive enclosure from which to repel an attack.[53]

The wagons employed were the standard U.S. Army M-1861, 6-mule Quartermaster Wagon, approximately 10' x 4.5' x 2.5' high. The corral was composed of fourteen of these wagon boxes, placed end-to-end so as to form an oval-shaped enclosure approximately 60-70' long by 25-30' wide, and extending, generally, from northeast to southwest. The space between each box was wide enough to permit a man to pass through, but too narrow for stock to escape.[54] The corral was positioned so that both "pineries" were under visual control and was "well selected for defense, and the best security that the country afforded for the stock."[55]

One wagon box with the canvas still attached to its bows, and in which was stored the rations for the civilian workers, was located near the east end of the enclosure, while a second wagon box, containing the army rations, was on the south side. Finally, one fully complete wagon (i.e., still mounted on its running gear), with reserve rations and bedding for the civilians was located some 10 feet from the west end of the corral. Both civilians and soldiers slept in tents pitched outside of the enclosure along its south side. Cooking was also done outside the corral, apparently on the west end.[56]

One of the earliest misconceptions of the Wagon Box Fight was that the boxes were lined with boiler iron, which would have rendered them bullet proof. Without exception, however, those participants who later described the fight all agreed that the boxes contained no metal lining and were constructed of nothing more than ordinary, inch-thick pine wood.

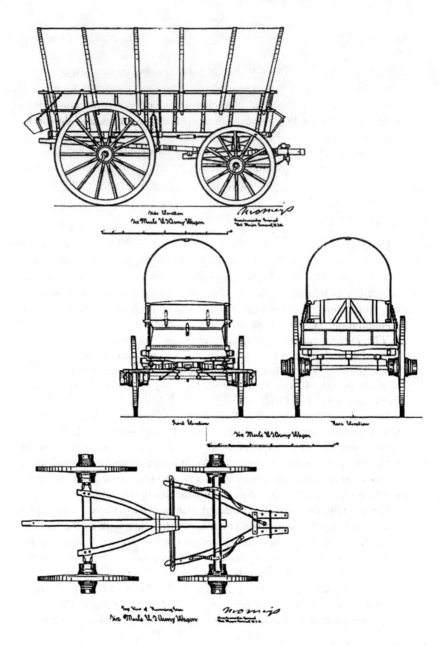

Some accounts have suggested that the boxes had loopholes bored in the sides, but there is no clear consensus on this point.[57]

During the month of July 1867, Company A, Twenty-seventh Infantry, had drawn the guard and escort assignment for the wood cutting operation but experienced little trouble from the Indians. The fact that there had been no real effort to harass the woodcutters during the early part of the summer was probably due to the Indians' preoccupation with their annual Sun Dance activities. However, with the conclusion of those ceremonials about the last week of July, the Sioux and some of their Cheyenne allies began discussing plans for an effort against the Bozeman Trail forts, but were apparently unable to agree on the target. One group apparently favored Fort Phil Kearny as the objective. However, the Cheyennes, led by warriors such as Dull Knife and Two Moons, favored an attack on Fort C. F. Smith. The end result was two war parties: one, composed mainly of Cheyennes, attacked the hay cutters at Fort C. F. Smith on August 1 in what is known as the Hayfield Fight. A second contingent struck Fort Phil Kearny's wood cutters and their escort the following day.[58]

The war party that attacked the wagon box corral consisted primarily of Oglalas under Crazy Horse and Miniconjous under High Back-Bone. A few Sans Arcs were also represented, as was a party of some 60 Cheyennes under Little Wolf.[59] Red Cloud is thought by some to have been on hand, but his presence cannot be verified.[60] The approximately 1,000 warriors comprising the Fort Kearny contingent departed from their Tongue and Rosebud River campsites, probably about July 31, and reached the general area of Piney Island on August 1, where they camped and made preparations to attack the wood cutters the following day.[61]

As a result of their triumph over Fetterman, the Indians were undoubtedly confident of another great victory. It is unclear whether the intent was to invite pursuit out of the fort by threatening the woodcutters, and luring the soldiers into another trap as they had done with Fetterman, or whether the effort was aimed at the woodcutters right from the start. However, if the Indians did indeed intend to repeat December's strategy, why did they not send a small party against the wood train, holding the main body back until the soldiers had taken the bait?[62]

In any case, on the afternoon of July 31, about the same time the Sioux war party was leaving its villages, Company C, Twenty-seventh Infantry, Captain James Powell commanding, departed Fort Phil Kearny under orders to relieve Company A. Powell's command numbered 51 enlisted men and one other officer, Lieutenant John C. Jenness. Company C was supplied with rations for 10 days and 150 rounds of ammunition per man.[63]

Standing five feet, eight inches tall, with brown hair and blue eyes, thirty-six-year-old James Powell was a Maryland-born army veteran with nineteen years of service, having enlisted as a private in 1848. At the outset of the Civil War he was promoted to second lieutenant, Eighteenth Infantry, the regiment in which he served throughout the Civil War. He was breveted for gallant and meritorious service at Chickamauga, and again at Jonesboro during the Atlanta Campaign, where he sustained two serious chest wounds. The lead from these wounds remained in Powell's body for the rest of his life and not surprisingly proved to be a continuing source of considerable discomfort.

Seated: John "Portugee" Phillips; standing: Capt. James Powell.
American Heritage Center, Univ. of WY

Powell was one of Colonel Henry Carrington's original officers, having come west with the Eighteenth Infantry in June 1866. Under the army's new plan of reorganization that had been authorized the previous July, but had not actually become effective until January 1, 1867, the second battalion, Eighteenth Infantry, which included Powell's Company C, became the new Twenty-seventh Infantry.[64]

Powell would retire from active duty in 1868 and survive until 1903 when he finally succumbed to the effects of his Civil War wounds, and to "general paresis," a disease of the brain caused by the effects of syphilis on the central nervous system. The disease may also have produced a form of insanity. Indeed, Powell's rather bizarre testimony during official inquiries in the wake of the Fetterman debacle caused some to question his mental capacity. There is, however, nothing at all to suggest that his judgment was in any way impaired on the day of the Wagon Box Fight.[65]

Powell's second-in-command, First Lieutenant John C. Jenness, was a native of Vermont. Like Powell, Jenness was a Civil War veteran who had come up through the ranks. He served first as an enlisted man in the Seventeenth New Hampshire Infantry, then was appointed lieutenant in the First New Hampshire Heavy Artillery. Jenness was mustered out at the end of the Civil War. A year later in 1866, he applied for a commission in the newly expanded Regular Army and was appointed second lieutenant in the Twenty-seventh Infantry. Jenness arrived at Fort Phil Kearny in February 1867, and in July of that year was assigned to Powell's Company C.[66]

Arriving at the wagon box corral, Powell discovered that the contractor's operation necessitated a division of his command. One noncommissioned officer and 13 men were given the job of escorting the wood train to and from the fort. Another non-commissioned officer and 12 men were assigned to guard the woodcutting camp, located "about one mile distant in a southwesterly direction, on a commanding point across the Little Piney Creek, at the foot of the mountains."[67] This second group was still further divided, with nine men being assigned to the main cutting party and the remaining four to the "side camp." These dispositions left Powell and Jenness with 24 men at the corral.[68]

It seems clear that at least a few Indians were already in the vicinity when Powell's command arrived at the corral. William Murphy, a member of Company A, recalled that on July 30, the day before Company C arrived, Indians had tried unsuccessfully to run off livestock grazing west of the corral. And on the night before the fight, Sam Gibson of Company C remembered how Private Jack McDonough's dog Jess seemed to sense that someone or something was lurking in the darkness beyond the sentinels.[69]

Lt. John C. Jenness
Little Bighorn Battlefield National Monument

Late in the afternoon of August 1, a loaded wood train arrived at the corral from the lower pinery and prepared to spend the night before continuing on to the fort. Reveille was sounded early on Friday, the second day of the month (known to the Lakotas as Moon of the Black Cherries). By sunrise, breakfast had been served, and shortly thereafter the loaded wood train and escort, commanded by Lieutenant Francis McCarthy, set out for Fort Phil Kearny. At the same time, an empty train headed back to the pinery for a refill, accompanied by its 13-man escort under the command of Corporal Riley Porter. Also in this group was John "Portugee" Phillips, who had ridden to Horseshoe Creek telegraph station and Fort Laramie with news of the Fetterman Disaster.[70]

And so the day began in rather routine fashion. Captain Powell reportedly went down to Little Piney Creek to take a bath.[71] Eighteen-year-old Private Sam Gibson, a five-foot, seven-inch, blue-eyed ex-shoemaker from Nottingham, England, known to his comrades as "Whitey," was appointed lance-corporal for the day and placed in charge of the picket post on the Little Piney.[72] A recent immigrant, Gibson had come to the U.S. with his family in 1865 and enlisted in the army the following year.[73]

Gibson's picket post was located on a small knoll, near the creek, about four hundred yards southwest of the corral, and roughly halfway between

the corral and the "side camp," which was located another 400 to 500 hundred yards farther to the southwest. An important consideration in choosing a location for the wagon box corral was the site's ability to provide good visual contact with the surrounding area. From the corral could be seen the sentry on Pilot Knob near Fort Phil Kearny, the "upper pinery," and the picket post on Little Piney.

The Lower Pinery side camp, however, could not be seen from the corral. Consequently, the picket

Sam Gibson in 1891.

American Heritage Center, University of WY

post near Little Piney Creek, manned on this day by Sam Gibson and his comrades, Privates Nolan Deming and John Garrett, provided a vital link in the operation's security by allowing the guards to maintain visual contact with both the side camp and the corral. Gibson recalled that upon arriving at the post he stuck willows in the ground and fashioned a makeshift canopy with his poncho for protection from the intense heat.[74]

About the time reveille was sounding at the wagon box corral, civilian teamster R. J. Smyth and a partner left Fort Phil Kearny to hunt deer in the nearby hills. Shortly after daylight, the pair "noticed a lot of Indian smoke signals on the hills, and decided that we had better get back to the fort." They soon discovered, however, that it would be safer to try and reach the wood train, then en route to the fort. This option, too, had to be discarded because Indians were discovered between them and the train. Smyth and his partner finally elected to try for the wagon box corral, which they barely managed to reach safely.[75]

Meanwhile, Gibson and Deming had been relaxing in the shade of their lean-to when Garrett spotted Indians and shouted an alarm. Off to the northwest, the three pickets saw seven mounted warriors moving single file at a dead run toward the Little Piney. Not yet having had an opportunity to try his new breech-loader, Sam Gibson adjusted the sights to 700 yards, laid the weapon on a stone breastwork, took careful aim, and fired. The bullet brought down the lead horse, whose rider was promptly picked up by one of his companions.[76]

Looking back to the northeast toward the corral and beyond, there were more Indians than the three pickets had ever seen at one time. Gibson directed Garrett to watch for signals from the corral, then sent Deming across the Little Piney to warn the choppers in the "side camp." While Deming was gone, his companions watched the Indians moving over the hills "like a big swarm of bees." As he viewed this unfolding—and unnerving—spectacle, Gibson grew increasingly uneasy because they had not received any signal to return to the corral. The situation was growing more threatening with each passing moment.[77]

Meanwhile, both the woodcutter's main camp and the side camp were already under attack. The Indians, having set fire to the wagons, forced the four choppers and their four-man escort to retreat toward the mountains. One of the choppers, J. I. Minnick, recalled that the biggest Indian in the group grabbed the whiskey jug, for which he was promptly shot by the leader of the choppers, a man named Jones. According to Minnick, the death of the big Indian "and the loss of the 'firewater' seemed to make the other Indians quite angry and eager for revenge."[78]

As Minnick's group fled toward the mountains, one of the soldiers was unable to keep up with the others and fell behind. Despite the covering fire provided by Minnick and another chopper, the soldier was caught and killed. Minnick was about to remind his companion that they would have to move quickly to save their own "skins," but glancing around, he discovered his companion had already run off, leaving his boots and rifle behind. Alone now, Minnick wasted no time heading up Little Piney. A short distance ahead he was relieved to see a friendly hand waving to him from behind a large mass of rocks.[79]

The other three choppers and one soldier had managed to escape and take refuge in these rocks. Minnick took a position next to the surviving soldier, whose curiosity soon proved to be his undoing. Raising his head just above the rocks, the soldier immediately drew fire from the Indians, one bullet striking uncomfortably close. Leader Jones admonished the man to keep his head down, but the soldier ignored the warning and shortly paid the price with a bullet between the eyes. Fortunately for Minnick's little group, the Indians lost interest in them, their attention having been diverted to the wagon box corral, where bigger things were shaping up.[80]

In the meantime, Deming returned to report on the action at the side camp, bringing a civilian herder along with him. Gibson concluded that their situation was critical and on his own volition, decided to abandon the picket post and return immediately to the corral. Accordingly, Gibson, Deming, and Garrett, accompanied by the civilian herder, started for the corral, pausing to fire as they ran. They had not traveled far, however, before Indians began swarming up out of the Little Piney Creek bottoms in twos and threes. Gibson recalled that one Sioux was waving an old Spencer carbine at his companions, urging them on. He and Gibson exchanged shots, with Gibson finally scoring a hit.[81]

The herder, who for some reason was leading his horse rather than riding, was evidently experiencing difficulty in getting the animal to step up the pace and asked Gibson to prod the creature with his bayonet. Gibson told the herder to forget the horse and start shooting, because the Indians seemed to be emerging from everywhere "like a flock of birds." Decked out in their finest war regalia, with bodies painted white, green, and yellow, Gibson remembered that it made them appear "hideous in the extreme."[82]

By this time the four men were running for their lives. Even the herder's horse, its rump and flanks bristling with arrows, seems to have decided that speed was of the essence. It was obvious to everyone that the Indians intended to intercept the little party before it reached the corral.

Max Littman
American Heritage Center, University of WY

However, at this critical juncture, there appeared yet another of the immigrant soldiers serving in the nineteenth-century frontier army. This one, a diminutive five-foot four-inch gray-eyed former German cigar-maker named Max Littman, dashed out from the corral, dropped down on one knee, and coolly began to deliver an effective covering fire that enabled Gibson and company to reach the corral, exhausted but safe.

WAGON BOX FIGHT. AUG. 2, 1867.

The wagon box corral, from a sketch furnished by Sam Gibson and later redrawn by Grace Hebard. The numbers represent the location of various participants. (1) Sam Gibson, (2) John Hoover, (3) Capt. Powell, (4) Max Littman, (5) James Condon, (6) Spot where Lieut. Jenness was killed (7&8) Bullwhackers in wagon boxes, (9) Where Private Doyle was killed, (10) Where Private Haggerty was killed, (11)Private John Somers wounded in wagon box. Big Piney Creek is to the north. *American Heritage Center, University of WY*

Like Gibson, the twenty-year-old Littman was a recent arrival in this country. Unlike Gibson, however, he could speak no English, though the language barrier in no way impeded his performance as a soldier. Indeed, he was already a corporal and within two months after the Wagon Box Fight would be promoted to sergeant. "He fought like a demon," Gibson later recalled.[83]

By the time Gibson and his companions reached the corral, Powell and Lieutenant Jenness had assembled the rest of the company. Ammunition was distributed, and the men were instructed to take up positions and be prepared to fight for their lives. Although relieved to be back at the corral, Gibson was also concerned at the repercussions that might result from abandoning the picket post without orders. Powell, however, assured the young soldier that he had "done nobly."[84]

In his official report, Powell said that "About 9 o'clock in the morning two hundred (200) Indians attacked the herders in charge of the herd, driving them off: at the same time some five hundred (500) attacked the train at the foot of the Mountains, driving off the men belonging there and burning it."[85]

In addition to the main body of defenders at the wagon box corral, three other groups were endangered by the Indian attack: the woodcutters, the wagon train and its escort, and the livestock herders. As we have seen, the woodcutters and their escort fled to the safety of the mountains, leaving burning wagons and equipage behind. However, the livestock herders—their number is unknown, but it was likely no more than three or four—were cut off, with Indians interposed between them and either the corral or the wood train. Seeing their plight, Powell allegedly sallied out of the corral with a small detachment and attacked the Indians from behind, creating a small diversion that enabled the herders to reach the safety of the wood train. Some of those who escaped into the mountains came into the corral after the fight, while others seem to have eventually made their way back to Fort Kearny.[86]

Powell had begun the day with a total of 53 men, including himself. However, better than fifty percent of his command—or 27 men—was on guard or escort duty and thus unavailable to participate in the defense of the corral. He had been reinforced by the addition of six civilians, including the teamster R. J. Smyth and his partner, so that the force in the corral numbered two officers, 24 enlisted men and six civilians, a total of 32 men.[87]

One can well imagine what it must have been like inside that corral as Powell's men prepared to defend themselves against an attack that was imminent: desperation on the faces of some, determination on others.

Gibson remembered that after the Fetterman disaster he had seen anger and revenge on men's faces, but today that had been replaced by looks of "intense earnestness and resolution." Surely, the fate of Fetterman's command, nearly three times the size of their own, must have weighed heavily on the minds of the defenders. Powell, in fact, later told his wife he never expected to get out alive, and young Sam Gibson—called the "kid" because of his youth—was warned by one of the older men that he would have to "fight like hell if he expected to come out alive." Some of the defenders made preparations to take their own lives in the event the corral was overrun, which loomed as a real possibility. Using their shoelaces, they fashioned a loop to fit around their foot. The other end was then attached to the trigger of their rifle. Should the position be overrun, it was only necessary to stand up, place the muzzle of the rifle under your chin and fire.[88]

Each man picked a spot that suited him best. Some prepared to fight from inside the wagon boxes, others from behind them. A few chose positions between the boxes, behind sacks of grain and oxen yokes. For once there was an adequate supply of ammunition and no shortage of weapons. The new Springfield breechloader was the predominant weapon on this day, though the civilians were also armed with other makes. Teamster Smyth recalled that he had two Spencer carbines and two Colt revolvers.[89]

The Indians did not immediately commence their attack on the corral. Instead, they made preparations to do so out of range, though not out of sight of the defenders. Watching them reminded Max Littman of two regiments of Prussian cavalry. After picking his spot, along the south wall of the corral, Sam Gibson joined a small party on the southwest quarter. The group included Lieutenant Jenness who was using field glasses to observe Indians massing in the valley of the Big Piney to the north of the corral and to the east around a high point, where he informed Powell he saw Red Cloud.[90] It must have been a brief hiatus, however, because Powell reported that within fifteen minutes after the initial attack on the mule herd and wood train, he "was surrounded by about eight hundred mounted Indians. . ."[91]

The Battlefield

Before proceeding with a reconstruction of the fight, a review of the battlefield locale is in order. No battle can be fully understood without an

Above: Looking east from the wagon box monument to the high point from where Red Cloud may have observed the fight. *Author photo*

Below: Looking southwest from the wagon box monument toward the ridge where Indian spectators watched the fight. *Ed Smyth*

exception. As will be explained later, the corral is believed to have extended along, roughly, a northeast-southwest axis, with some portion projecting beyond the present fence that encloses state property. The irrigation ditch running along the eastern periphery did not exist at the time of the fight. However, the drop-off north of the corral did exist and was a key terrain factor. The drop-off actually commences at a point about 60 yards east of the present marker and extends around to the north and west, in the shape of a fishhook, before ending some two hundred yards west of the monument. At its closest point it is about 35 yards from the corral. The rim of this drop-off would later provide excellent cover for Indian marksmen, who would be responsible for most of the casualties inflicted on the corral's defenders.[92]

To the south-southwest, the land is an open plain, running several hundred yards to Little Piney Creek. West of the present monument, the land also stretches unbroken for several hundred yards to the high land mass that later served as a gathering point for Indian spectators. East of the monument, approximately 700-750 yards, is yet another high point that also played a role in the drama that was about to unfold. It was on this hill that Jenness thought he spotted Red Cloud.

The Fight at the Corral

The First Attack

As the Indians launched their first attack, Powell instructed his men to "shoot to kill," and apparently issued few other orders throughout the fight, the demands of the hour apparently being self-evident.[93]

Some disagreement exists as to the method and direction of the initial attack. According to Private Gibson, it was a mounted charge from the open plain between Big and Little Piney Creeks, which could only mean the southwest because this is the only area expansive enough to serve as a staging ground for a large body of mounted warriors. This tends to be supported by Captain Powell, who said that he was "surrounded by about eight hundred (800) *mounted* [italics added] warriors." Max Littman, however, recalled that the first attack came from the north and was made by warriors on foot. In point of fact, Littman claims that *all* [italics added] of the attacks he witnessed were made by warriors on foot.[94] This discrepancy is difficult to explain, particularly since Littman and Gibson would have had essentially the same view of the fight.[95]

The three extant descriptions of this opening phase of the fight were recorded by Powell, Gibson, and Littman. On the face of it, Powell's and Gibson's appear to be at odds with Littman's version. However, the disparity may not be as great as it initially seems to be. According to Powell,

> . . . Some fifteen minutes afterwards (after the initial strike on the woodcutters and livestock herders) I was surrounded by about eight hundred (800) mounted Indians. . . .

Although Powell does not go on to specifically describe the initial attack in terms of its direction, or whether it was mounted or on foot, the *implication* is that it was a mounted attack.[96]

Gibson's account is similar:

> . . .The whole plain was alive with Indians, all mounted and visible in every direction. They were riding madly about, and shooting at us with guns, bows and arrows, first on one side and then on the other of the corral. . . .[97]

Littman's recollection seems to be strikingly different that those presented by Powell and Gibson:

> . . . All the charges that I saw made against us by the Indians were on foot. True, they were on their ponies when they came down the mountain-sides and across the country, but the ponies were left out of rifle range, and the squaws to attend them, and the advances were all made without them—at least all that came under my observation. . . .
> The first advance against us was made from the north. Many of the Indians circled us on their ponies and shot arrows into the corral in this manner, but they did not make a direct charge on horseback. . . .[98]

A closer examination of the accounts offered by Gibson and Littman reveals that they are not so dissimilar after all. Each man remembered the Indians circling on horseback and loosing arrows or spears at the corral. But they seem to part company when Littman goes on to talk about the Indians leaving their ponies behind and attacking on foot. Littman, in point of fact, positively refutes the idea of a direct charge on horseback. Yet we know from the other accounts that indeed warriors on horseback were involved in the opening attacks.[99]

It may be that the sticking point here concerns the definition of a "mounted charge." To Gibson and others, the threatening moves by warriors on horseback may have seemed like a mounted charge, but others, like Max Littman, clearly did not see it as such.

The real discrepancy in these accounts, however, is Littman's statement that the first advance was from the north. Given Littman's position in the corral—southwest quarter by his own admission—approximately 25-35 feet to the right of Sam Gibson, with essentially the same view of events, makes his statement difficult to reconcile. Perhaps in recalling the fight later, Littman simply got his directions reversed—an easy enough thing to do. It should also be pointed out that, with the exception of Powell's official report (and that of Major Smith who commanded the relief column), these accounts were all recorded many years after the event and, as will be seen later, in the controversy surrounding the location of the corral itself, memory must be used with caution.[100]

There is no evidence that Powell attempted to use any kind of fire control in repelling the Indian attacks, although some accounts suggest that only the better marksmen actually fired, while the others tended to the business of reloading.[101] Sam Gibson recalled that the attackers rode back and forth, each time coming a bit closer. "Then," explained Gibson, "they would circle, and each time come in closer, uttering the most piercing and unearthly war cries. Some of the more venturesome would ride in close and throw spears at us."[102]

It bears noting that Indian battle tactics differed greatly from those of the soldiers. Indians fought as individuals; there was no formal organization, no unified plan of attack, at least not insofar as those concepts were understood by the white man. It might be that a decoy-ambush stratagem would be planned for a particular situation—such as apparently was the case with Fetterman—and warriors would be exhorted to restrain themselves and not spring the trap prematurely, but they often did anyway. An Indian war party operated as a body of very loosely organized individuals acting toward a common cause, as opposed to soldiers who fought as a tightly organized body, governed by strict rules of deployment. In battle, an Indian warrior might choose to follow a particular war chief whose medicine was believed to be strong, but he was essentially on his own. He was, in a very real sense, his own general.

With this in mind, and using the descriptions of Gibson and Littman, an image of the battle's opening phase begins to take shape: the corral is endangered by a large number of Indians on all quarters, but mainly from the south-southwest. Many are on horseback, galloping back and forth in a threatening manner, perhaps hoping to lure the soldiers out to fight in the open. Others are on foot. All are gesturing, yelling, firing arrows, or discharging a firearm if they had one. In return, they draw fire from the defenders in the corral. And then, suddenly, there is the swell of a general

Artist Theodore Pitman relied heavily on Sam Gibson's recollections in creating this depiction of the Wagon Box Fight. The view shows the defenders facing south and west—*American Heritage Center, University of WY*

forward movement, mostly by mounted warriors from the south-southwest. But there is activity elsewhere around the corral's perimeter as well, as Indians on foot crawl forward, sniping with rifle and bow from just behind the rim of the drop-off on the north. The attackers are met by a steady blast

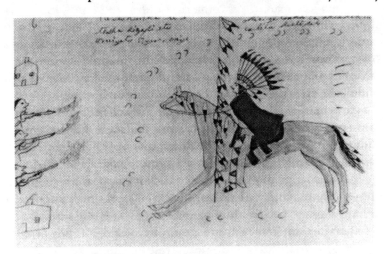

White Bull's pictograph of the Wagon Box Fight. *Elwyn B. Robinson Dept. of Special Collections, University of North Dakota*

The fight as sketched by A. Nicolai, 2d Cavalry. This sketch, apparently, was later presented to Frederick Claus. *American Heritage Center, University of WY*

of fire from the defenders. There are casualties, probably more than expected. The Indians fall back, surprised by the steady volume of fire. The usual pause in firing while the soldiers reloaded had been missing. Probably surprised by the steady volume of fire that poured forth from the corral, the Indians finally pulled back. "Finding they could not enter the corral," Powell wrote, "they retired to a hill about six hundred yards distant and there stripped for more determined fighting."[103]

There is no way to tell how many Indians had firearms, but evidently more than a few possessed them.[104] William Murphy of Company A believed that until the new breech-loaders arrived, the Indians were better armed than the soldiers. Sam Gibson recalled that behind the north drop-off, "Indians on foot had placed themselves in scores, all armed with rifles." Gibson also described how the "tops of the wagon beds were literally ripped and torn to slivers by their bullets." Max Littman, too, remembered the Indians being well armed.[105]

There is nothing to indicate just how long the first attack lasted, but it probably seemed longer to the defenders than it was in actuality. There was little conversation during the brief hiatus that followed the opening attack. Gibson called the silence "uncanny." Some crawled over to replenish their supply of ammunition from one of the seven boxes that Powell had directed be placed around the corral. Many used their forage caps to hold

Frederick Claus
Margie Claus Duppong

cartridges. The mood inside the corral was one of grim resolution. "We did not know what time it was," explained Gibson, "and nobody cared."

Meanwhile, on the other side of the corral, the Indians, some mounted, others on foot, dashed in to recover their dead and wounded. Some crawled forward behind the protection of buffalo hide shields and dragged dead and wounded back with them. Others, in a superb display of horsemanship, dashed in, grabbed a wounded comrade by the wrist or hand, and carried him to safety. Both Gibson and Littman also noted that the Indians used mirrors to communicate.[106]

Some Indians watched the battle from a high point west of the corral. Powell reported that the "hills in the immediate vicinity were covered with Indians who merely acted as spectators, until they saw how fruitless were the efforts of their comrades near my corral when they also moved up, and seemed determined to carry my position at all hazards and massacre my command."[107]

There were two non-combatant occupants of the corral: a mule and pony tied to one of the wagon boxes on the west end of the corral. An estimated dozen arrows managed to strike the pony, which eventually had to be shot. Disturbed by fire arrows that were landing too close, the mule began to "raise Hell and his heels at the same time," recalled Gibson, and he finally had to be shot as well.[108]

The Fight at the Corral

The Second Attack

After evaluating the situation, the Indians launched their second major effort, which again seems to have been primarily by mounted warriors along an arc of 180 degrees from the east to south to west, although there continued to be activity by snipers along the north wall as well. As the attackers surged forward toward the corral, someone realized that the tents outside the enclosure blocked the line of fire. These tents should have been taken down at the outset of the engagement, and why they were not is unknown. In any event, Gibson, Private John Grady, and some others now made a dash for the tents and managed to "drop" all but the one used by Powell.[109] With the tents out of the way, the defenders had a clear field of vision and proceeded to pour a steady stream of fire at the oncoming Indians. Gibson recalled that many gun barrels became overheated from the intense firing. The well known mountain man Jim Baker added to his tall-tale reputation when he later told Fort Phil Kearny's commanding officer, Colonel John Smith, that he ". . .kept eight rifles red hot and with a rest I can hit a silver dollar every shot at a hundred yards."[110]

During this second attack, Indian snipers secreted behind the rim along the northwest perimeter killed Lieutenant Jenness and Privates Henry Haggerty, and Tommy Doyle, who had been Sam Gibson's "bunkie" when the regiment marched across the plains during the summer of 1866.[111]

Jenness and four civilians had been fighting from a standing position inside the two covered wagon boxes. This particular pair of wagons (which apparently belonged to the civilian contractor) were of a different construction than the others, with higher sides offering a little more protection, though in Jenness's case it mattered not. Warned to keep down, Jenness reportedly replied, "I know how to fight Indians," and promptly fell over dead from a bullet in the forehead. After Jenness was killed, Max Littman attempted to drag the dead mule over to protect the lieutenant's body from further damage by bullets and arrows, but found the carcass too heavy and was forced to give up.[112]

Under a brassy August sun, the acrid odor of expended gunpowder, mingled with the stench of smoldering hay and manure ignited by fire arrows, combined to create a terrible thirst among the defenders. The smudge from the smoldering hay and manure, mingled with the pall of black powder smoke from the new Springfield breech-loaders, added to the defenders' discomfort.[113] One water barrel only 20 feet from the west end of the corral had been hit several times, so that nearly all of the water had leaked out. However, under the covered wagon, 100 feet beyond the northwest end, hung a pair of camp kettles containing the breakfast cooking water. Once again, Sam Gibson and John Grady volunteered. The two were given covering fire, but it remained a risky proposition. Happily, they managed to bring back the kettles without being hit themselves, but when Gibson looked at his kettle he found it leaking from two holes. Fortunately, sufficient water remained in both vessels to last through the remainder of the fight.[114]

Among the Indians attacking on foot, displaying great personal courage, was an unusually large warrior brazenly brandishing a spear, buffalo-hide shield, and chanting a war song. He seems also to have been armed with bow and arrows because as he advanced, the Indian dodged about, now and then leaping into the air, releasing an arrow at the apex of his leap. Several of the defenders tried unsuccessfully to get him, but it was young Max Littman who finally brought him down. Littman remembered this as a personal duel between the big Indian and himself.[115]

Meanwhile, back at Fort Kearny, Colonel Jonathan Smith had been made aware of Powell's plight. If there was a picket on Pilot Knob that day, he would surely have seen the smoke, and the wood train would certainly have brought word of the fight as well. Moreover, as noted in Major Smith's official report, the Indians also made a demonstration at the fort itself and this alone may have been sufficient cause for Colonel Smith to send a relief party to the pinery.[116]

Major Benjamin Smith was immediately ordered to proceed to the scene with a relief party. "Yesterday about Guard Mounting," he remembered,

> hostile Indians made their appearance on all sides of the Post. At first just a few but gradually increasing to several hundred. About 11:00 a.m. developments indicated that the wood Party and its guard, five

miles in the Pinery were in imminent danger. Bvt. Maj. Gen John E. Smith Commanding, directed me to proceed to their relief with Lieutenants Connolly, Paulus and McCarthy of the 27th Inf. and one hundred enlisted men of the same Regiment from Companies A and F. I also took a Mountain Howitzer and ten ox wagons, the citizen teamsters being armed. My command started about 11:30 a.m. and proceeded cautiously to the Pinery with skirmishers and flankers thrown out.[117]

By the time Smith's column departed from Fort Kearny, Powell's command had been engaged for about three hours, and from all indications it had turned back at least two major efforts against the corral. Indeed, Max Littman recalled that the corral withstood eight charges "between 7 o'clock and 1:30 o'clock on all sides of the fort." The Sioux, however, were far from discouraged.[118] On the open plain to the south and west, mounted warriors galloped back and forth, some brandishing spears, others now and again firing at the corral. One defender believed he saw two Indians wearing the coats of Fetterman and Brown.[119]

Before long Powell's men heard a new sound. It grew in intensity until suddenly, from behind the rim along the northwest perimeter, a large body of warriors on foot burst onto the plateau. The attack was led by a magnificently war-bonneted individual, said to have been Red Cloud's nephew. The warriors, shouting their songs of war, fired with determination and surged toward the corral. The sight "chilled my blood," remembered Sam Gibson.

Powell's men, however, responded to this attack just as they had the earlier ones—shooting as fast as they could reload. Among those hit was the one alleged to be Red Cloud's nephew. Exactly how close the Indians got to the wagons is difficult to say. According to Littman, "They advanced to within two hundred feet of the corral." Gibson remembered they were close enough to "see the whites of their eyes . . . so close that it seemed as if nothing could prevent their swarming over our barricade and into our corral."[120]

However close they came, the effort fell short. The fire from the corral was heavy and nearly continuous. Almost certainly the defenders who had been stationed on the south rampart joined their comrades along the north wall, so we may assume that the attackers were exposed to the maximum firepower of Powell's command. Accordingly, confronted by what must have been a withering blast, the Indians, not surprisingly, broke off the attack and withdrew. Interestingly enough, Gibson noted that during the attack on the north and northwest sections of the corral the mounted warriors on the open plain to the south merely watched the proceedings, but provided no support.[121]

Following the repulse of the assault on the north wall, some of the defenders, believing that Red Cloud was amongst a group on the high hill to the east of the corral, raised the sights on their rifles and fired several volleys, reportedly scoring a few hits.[122]

It was now nearing 1:00 p.m., and some of the defenders on the south and west noted that several hostiles on one of the nearby hills suddenly dispersed and went galloping down the valley. A shout went up from the east end of the corral, triumphantly announcing the arrival of the relief column. The deep-throated "boom" of Major Smith's mountain howitzer rang out across the countryside. The artillery and arrival of reinforcements scattered the remaining Indians, who apparently had little stomach to continue the struggle—especially now that more soldiers were on the scene. Max Littman later said that the shell from the howitzer scattered some 400-500 Indians assembling on the hill *north* of the corral and preparing to charge. Littman is almost certainly in error, however, and he must have meant the high hill to the east of the corral.[123]

In his official report of what came to be known as the Wagon Box Fight, Major Smith described the arrival of his column:

> On nearing the corral of the Wood Party and about a mile and a half from it, I discovered that a high hill near the road and overlooking the corral of the Wood Party was occupied by a large party of Indians, in my estimation, five or six hundred were in sight, many more probably concealed. The grass was burning in every direction. The Indians appearing disposed to make a stand I turned off the road to the right, some few hundred yards, to occupy the extreme right point of the hill, which was flanked on that side by a steep precipice, with the intention after securing it to follow.' the ridge to the corral of the Wood Party, commanded by Bvt. Maj. Powell, 27th Inf. Before turning from the road in obedience to my instructions, I fired a shot from the Howitzer, as a signal to inform Bvt. Maj. Powell's command that assistance was near. The shell fired was in the direction of the Indians, but fell short as anticipated, but seemed to disconcert them as a number of mounted Indians who were riding rapidly toward my command turned and fled. Upon my ascending to the crest of the hill all had disappeared from it and were seen across the creek on an opposite hill about of a mile away leaving all clear to Bvt. Major Powell's corral.[124]

To say that Powell's men offered a warm welcome to the relief column would be a decided understatement. They jumped into the air, shouted, hugged each other, laughed, cried, and generally exhibited the sort of behavior that might be expected from a group of men who had suddenly been granted a reprieve from a hideous death. As a result of the smoke from their guns, William Murphy thought that the defenders looked as though they had "used burnt cork on their faces." The post surgeon, Doctor Samuel P. Horton, who had accompanied Smith's column, received Powell's permission to give each man a drink of whiskey.[125]

Shortly after Smith's arrival, four choppers and fourteen soldiers came into the corral, having hidden out in the foothills during the fighting. Smith dispatched a company under Lieutenant Thomas Connolly to check for other survivors in the pinery. His investigation found nothing but burned and abandoned wagons. The four surviving choppers from the side camp remained in hiding until late that night, by which time they were so overcome with thirst they elected to risk sneaking back to the fort. J. I. Minnick, one of the choppers, was the only one who seems to have kept his boots. By the time the four men reached Fort Phil Kearny at 5:00 a.m. the following morning, the other three had such sore feet that they were barely able to walk for several days.[126]

Not wishing to give the Sioux an opportunity to resume the attack, Smith and Powell wasted no time heading back to Fort Phil Kearny. Upon reaching the high point east of the corral that had served as the Indians' field headquarters, they looked back and saw a line of Indian ponies carrying off dead and wounded.[127] Evidently, the Indians were unable to retrieve all of their dead and wounded, however, because some of the soldiers returned to the fort with scalps and one Indian "head," which Surgeon Horton subsequently sent to Washington for examination.[128]

Casualties

Given the intensity of the fight, Powell's losses were light: just three killed and two wounded in the corral itself, and three others killed in the fight at the side camp.[129] Indian losses, as in so many other engagements, are virtually impossible to determine with any real accuracy. Assessments range from an unlikely low of two to an absurd high of 1,500. Powell estimated that "there were not less than sixty Indians killed on the spot and one hundred twenty severely wounded." Gibson, Littman, and other defenders imply that Powell's estimate was extremely conservative. At least one Indian account, that of the Oglala Sioux warrior Fire Thunder, seems to support the claim that Indian losses were relatively heavy. According to Fire Thunder, there were "dead warriors and horses piled all around the boxes and scattered over the plain."[130]

Those who have studied the event from the Indian perspective, however, agree that army casualty reports are wildly exaggerated. In view of the fact that Powell's men had not had time to test fire their new breechloaders, and allowing for the fact that most of the defenders were highly excited and many probably fired wildly, it is entirely possible that even Powell's estimate was too high.[131]

What was more important in the final analysis was that the Springfield-Allin breech-loaders represented the difference between survival and a repeat of the Fetterman fight. Major Smith was of the opinion that "if Powell's men had been armed with muzzle-loaders instead of breech-loaders, his party would have been massacred before my arrival."[132]

The significance of the Wagon Box Fight was two-fold: first it reaffirmed a long established tenet that a small and well armed defensive force, fighting from a strong position, often enjoyed a tactical advantage over a numerically superior foe. It was a scenario that would be repeated at Beecher Island in 1868, and again at Adobe Walls in 1874.

Second, and perhaps most important, at least to the garrison at Fort Phil Kearny, the Wagon Box victory restored a measure of prestige and confidence to a frontier army whose self-esteem was at a low ebb.

Psychologically, the Wagon Box Fight was as much a tonic to the U.S. Army as the Fetterman Fight had been to the Indians.

Chapter 3

The Site Controversy

An intriguing sidelight of the Wagon Box Fight is the controversy regarding the exact location of the corral. Two sites are involved. The official and most visible of the two is the fenced-in enclosure containing the large rock monument, and a small granite marker, located a short distance to the northeast. This site is located in Sheridan County, approximately one mile south of the little community of Story. The access road to this site also happens to be the boundary line between Sheridan and Johnson Counties. Just across the line in Johnson County, some five hundred yards southeast of the large monument is a four-inch iron pipe that also marks what is believed by some to be the site of the wagon box corral.

The Origins of the Controversy

The controversy surrounding these two sites seems to have originated in 1908, when Sam Gibson came out to Sheridan to join General and Mrs. Carrington and others in dedicating the Fetterman monument. Desiring to revisit the scene of the Wagon Box Fight, Gibson, in the company of a local citizen, Charles E. Bezold, headed out to the area. En route, however, Gibson was either kicked or thrown by his horse, and in any case injured his leg so that he felt unable to finish the journey. However, they did get close

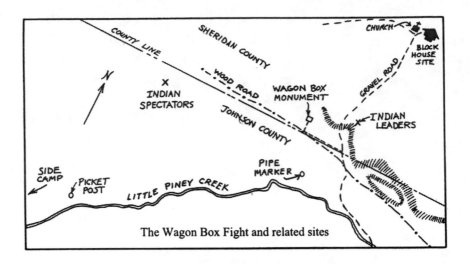

The Wagon Box Fight and related sites

enough for Gibson to point out various landmarks and advise Bezold that if he would look in a certain spot he would find shell casings that would identify the location of the corral.[133]

Bezold was unable to undertake a search for two weeks, at which time he returned to the area and did indeed find shell casings, just as Gibson had predicted. Bezold apparently did nothing with the shells at the time, but several years later he sent them to Grace Raymond Hebard, Secretary of the Historical Landmarks Commission at the University of Wyoming. Dr. Hebard had the shells examined and was subsequently advised that they were definitely of the type used in the Wagon Box Fight.[134]

In view of this, the Landmarks Commission decided to invite Gibson back to Sheridan to take part in dedicating a permanent marker to be erected on the spot where Bezold found the shell casings. However, because of various World War I activities, the visit had to be postponed and it was not until late July 1919 that Gibson was able to return for another visit. Together, Gibson and Bezold walked and drove through the area, with Gibson pointing out various landmarks. Eventually, Gibson went to the spot where he remembered the wagon box corral to have been located and once again shell casings were found.[135]

Meanwhile, in 1916, in conjunction with a celebration commemorating the fortieth anniversary of the Battle of the Little Bighorn, an interested group gathered in Sheridan for the purpose of visiting historical sites in the area. In addition to its organizer, Walter Mason Camp, the 21-man party included General Edward S. Godfrey, a survivor of the Little Bighorn, noted anthropologist Dr. George Bird

Left: Walter Camp's pipe marker, believed by some to mark the site of the wagon box corral. The location is approximately 500 yards southeast of the large monument seen in the top center of the photo. *Ed Smyth*

Below: A close-up view of the pipe marker. *Ed Smyth*

Grinnell, and Major James McLaughlin, the Chief Inspector for the Indian Bureau.[136]

Camp had previously obtained separate interviews with both Sam Gibson and Max Littman regarding the location of the wagon box corral. Using Camp's notes as a guide, the group carefully examined the area and finally settled on the spot where the pipe marker now stands. Three days later, on the morning of June 30, 1916, Mr. H. C. Benham, president of the Sheridan Commercial Club, and Mr. H. H. Thompson, editor of *The Teepee Book*, returned to the site and planted the four-inch iron pipe, capped with a six-inch brass plate that reads "Site of the WAGON BOX FIGHT Aug. 2, 1867."[137]

Six weeks later, on August 15, 1916, Max Littman also paid a visit to the area. The party included his wife and daughter, as well as Walter

An early view of the pipe marker. *American Heritage Center, University of WY*

Camp, H. H. Thompson, and T. C. Diers, a Sheridan, Wyoming, banker. After carefully studying the lay of the land, Littman—reportedly without any prompting—chose the site of Camp's pipe marker. Although Camp's choice was based on information supplied by recollections offered by Gibson and Littman, it should be remembered that Camp's original interview with them was not conducted on the site. Littman's unprompted selection of Camp's site afterward clarified nothing and indeed only served to muddy the waters.[138]

That fall, Grace Hebard, who had begun to develop a deep interest in the Wagon Box Fight, visited the Fort Phil Kearny area. In company with a small party that included Charles E. Bezold, Dr. Hebard went to the area where Bezold, pursuant to Gibson's instructions, found cartridges eight years earlier. Hebard and her party examined the ground closely and located a number of artifacts, including a piece of wood that subsequently proved to be from one of the water buckets used at the corral. Additionally, Hebard discovered a circle of stones that Sam Gibson later explained was where the men had built a coffee fire.[139]

As a result of her findings, Hebard was convinced that the Camp marker was incorrectly located. Accordingly, in 1919, she paid Sam Gibson eighty-five dollars in travel expenses (out of her own funds) to come out and once more go over the ground to determine where the wagon box corral had been located. Gibson accepted and in August of that year returned to Sheridan. Again he traveled to the site with Charles Bezold.

Above: Grace Raymond Hebard discussing the location of the wagon box corral with three companions. *American Heritage Center, University of* WY

Below: Charles Bezold drives the tie spike marking the location of the wagon box corral in 1919. The man in the black suit and hat is Sam Gibson. The Oregon Trail Commission under Grace Raymond Hebard's supervision, later erected the small granite marker on this site. It lies a short distance to the northeast of the large monument. *American Heritage Center, University of WY*

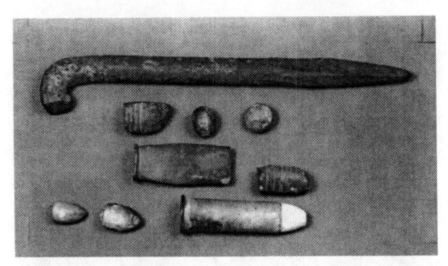

Artifacts from the wagon box fight. Top: iron, hand-forged tent pin. Second row: .58-caliber Minie ball (incoming); a fired .52-caliber Indian ball (incoming); Third row: fired .50-70-450 cartridge case (Martin Bar-Anvil, C1866-68); fired .50-70-450 bullet, 3-groove rifling, Springfield M1866, 2d Allin conversion (outgoing); Bottom row: .36-caliber conical ball (U.S.) (fired outgoing); .44-caliber conical ball (U.S.) (fired outgoing); live, unfired .50-70-450 cartridge (Martin Bar-Anvil). *H. Sterling Fenn Collection*

(Hebard was not present.) As he had done eleven years earlier, Gibson pointed out landmarks and vividly recalled the battle he had participated in 52 years earlier.

This time, however, he and Bezold examined the ground more carefully. At the conclusion of their study, Gibson selected the area where the large marker now stands and where Bezold had originally found shell casings. Gibson also marked the site and a "large railroad tie spike was driven into the ground at that point."[140]

In 1920, John Hoover, another surviving participant, visited the scene of the fight as part of yet another group excursion. After studying the terrain, Hoover selected a spot close to Littman's site. Later, Hoover seemed to change his mind, telling Hebard that he thought she didn't have the exact place, "but probably was within 40 feet of where he had located it."[141]

Unfairly perhaps, and no doubt unintentionally, the two proponents, Camp and Hebard, wound up pitting two old veterans against each other. Ironically, once before on this same field, Max Littman had come to Whitey Gibson's aid. This time, however, they were on opposing sides.

Despite the presence of battle artifacts discovered at the Gibson site (the present large rock marker), Walter Camp remained unconvinced and refused to accept the Hebard–Gibson findings, as did T. C. Diers, who, in point of fact, had serious reservations about Gibson's "mental condition."[142]

When asked about the pipe marker, Gibson explained that he had given information to Camp in Omaha while the latter was en route to Sheridan. Gibson had attempted to describe the location of the corral as best he could from memory and diagrams. Gibson remarked that he was pleased that his description had enabled Camp to come as close as he did.[143]

In September 1920, the Oregon Trail Commission placed a granite marker on the spot where Sam Gibson had seen his tie spike driven into the ground the year before, and where Hebard and her party had discovered artifacts four years earlier. Hebard received additional reinforcement for her choice in 1929 when Samuel Porter, son of J. R. Porter, who had been the civilian wood contractor at the time of the fight, told her that his father had selected the site for the corral. There was no question about it, maintained Porter: it was located where the present granite monument is found today.[144]

In addition to the large rock monument and pipe marker sites, one other location has been suggested. This third site, consisting of the remains of a large circular entrenchment, approximately 300 yards west by south of the monument, was erected by Lieutenant Alexander Wishart as a defensive position in the immediate aftermath of the fight. When queried about this site, Gibson again pointed out that the original corral contained no entrenchments, and that this was the site of the corral selected *after* the fight. Moreover, no battle artifacts of any kind have been found at the Wishart Corral.[145]

In 1936, seventeen years after Gibson's identification of the site, the CCC (Civilian Conservation Corps) under the direction of the Sheridan Chamber of Commerce, erected the large rock monument. This marker now stands at what was approximately the west edge of the corral, which actually extended to the east, beyond the present fence. The Oregon Trail Commission marker is located a short distance to the northeast of the large monument and sits just inside the fence.[146]

But that, it seems, was not to be the end of the controversy. In an article appearing in the September 1950 issue of the *Chicago Westerner's Brand Book*, the late T. J. Gatchell, a Buffalo, Wyoming, druggist and amateur historian, pointed out that Camp, with the assistance of Max Littman and John Hoover, had correctly identified the pipe marker as the site of the corral. In an effort to lend more credence to the pipe marker argument, Gatchell stated that, even before Camp's survey, he had visited the site with one Frank Peach, a bullwhacker who had participated in the fight. Peach, too, verified the pipe marker as the correct location of the wagon box corral.[147]

The marker commemorating the Wagon Box Fight. *Author photo*

Some years after the erection of the large monument, Gatchell again visited the area, this time with his friend Medicine Bear, a Cheyenne chief. When Medicine Bear inquired if Gatchell wished to know where the soldiers or Indians had been located, Gatchell replied that he wished to know about the soldiers, whereupon Medicine Bear climbed through the fence and promptly proceeded to within ten feet of Camp's pipe marker.[148]

Conclusions

The choice of both sites was heavily influenced by the personal recollections of two aging survivors, each with his supporters.[149] As time went on, and Gibson and Littman passed from the scene, those who had championed one or the other stood firm and the controversy persisted.

There is, however, evidence of a non-personal nature that confirms the choice of the present rock monument as the place of the fight. First, a crucial consideration in selecting the corral site was the need to maintain visual contact with both pineries *and the picket post,* neither of which can be seen from the pipe marker site because it is approximately 26 feet lower in elevation than the rock monument.[150]

The archeological evidence is also telling. Empty shells have been found at both sites, but those found at the pipe marker were not manufactured until *after* the Wagon Box Fight. The shells found in the vicinity of the rock monument were of the inside-primed, center-fire, Martin bar-anvil type—the only shell that had been manufactured for use in the Springfield-Allin breech-loaders used at the Wagon Box Fight. Shells found at the pipe marker site, on the other hand, had the Benet-cup primer that was not produced until *after* 1868. Because of this, and in the absence of any hard evidence to support it as the correct location, it simply is not possible to muster a compelling argument for the pipe marker site.

Thus, it seems clear that the large rock marker represents the approximate location of the wagon box corral.[151]

Appendix A

The Official Reports

Official Reports
Major Benjamin E. Smith
Captain James Powell

Ft. Philip Kearny, D.T.
August 3, 1867

Sir:

In compliance with [indecipherable] orders from the Bvt. Major General commanding, I have the honor to make the following report of operations of my command sent to relieve the wood party which was supposed to be in danger from a large party of hostile Indians showing themselves in the vicinity of the post.

Yesterday about Guard Mounting, hostile Indians made their appearance on all sides of the post, at first a few, but gradually increasing to several hundred. About 11 o'clock developments indicated that the Wood Party and its guard five miles in the Pinery were in imminent danger. Bvt Maj. Gen'l John E. Smith, Comd'g directed me to proceed to their relief with Lieutenants Connolly, Paulus and McCarthy of the 27th Inf. And one hundred Enlisted men of the same regiment from Companies "A" and "F."

I also took a Mountain howitzer and ten ox wagons, the citizen teamsters being armed. My command started about 11:30 a.m. and proceeded cautiously to the Pinery with skirmishers and flankers thrown out. On nearing the corral of the Wood Party and about a mile and a half from it, I discovered that a high hill near the road and overlooking the corral of the Wood Party was occupied by a large party of Indians, in my estimation five or six hundred were in sight, many more probably concealed. The grass was burning in every direction. The Indians appearing disposed to make a stand I turned off the road to the right, some few hundred yards, to occupy the extreme right point of the hill, which was flanked on that side by a steep precipice, with the intention of securing it to follow the ridge to the corral of the Wood Party, commanded by Bvt. Maj. Powell, 27th Inf. Before turning from the road in obedience to instructions, I fired a shot from the Howitzer, as a signal to inform Bvt. Major Powell's command that assistance was near. The shell fired was in the direction of the Indians, but fell short, as I anticipated, but seemed to disconcert them as a number of mounted Indians who were riding rapidly toward my command turned and fled. Upon my ascending to the crest of the hill all had disappeared from it and were seen across the creek, on an opposite hill about   of a mile away leaving all clear to Bvt. Major Powell's corral. Arriving there I saw evidence of a stubborn and severe fight. The wagon bodies were riddled with bullets, and a large number of [word is undecipherable, but possibly animals] were found in the corral. Lt. Jenness and two soldiers had been killed and two soldiers wounded. I also saw the dead bodies of [three?] Indians which had been left on the ground. The oxen were all gone. Major Powell gave me a description of his fight, but as he will make a written report, I will not detail it. I found his force inside the corral in strength about 24. Four citizen wood choppers and soldiers, numbering about 14, came into the corral after my arrival, having abandoned their wagons in the woods. They had been driven away by the Indians who took possession of the [word is undecipherable, but possibly corral or cattle] and destroyed the wagons. In reporting to me, these men were said to be about three miles from the corral. And none were hurt. Although this small corral of [several?] wagons belonging to Mr. [word is undecipherable, but the name is possibly Weston] was about a mile and a half from Major Powell's. No one coming in from it, I sent Lieut. Connolly with his Company to ascertain its state, he returned, reporting the wagons burned [remainder of the sentence appears to read "all ___ _____ _____ and cattle? gone]. No evidence of anyone killed or wounded there, it afterwards appeared that these men fled to the Mountains. Four returned to the Post before my command, and a few are still missing, supposed to have been killed. After carefully placing the dead and wounded of Maj. Powell's command in the Wagons, and loading all the most valuable articles we were able to carry, I abandoned Every thing [sic] Else, and in accordance with my instructions, <u>all</u> returned to the Post and without further [encountering?] no Indians.

I will give it as my opinion that if Major Powell's men had been armed with Muzzle, instead of breech loaders that his party would have been massacred before my arrival.

In this connection I will again refer to the indifference and careless use of citizen owners and wagon masters of trains, and stock in this most dangerous of all the Indian country. The fact of constantly herding this stock too far out in Exposed places, and in this particular case of the Weston's train, being a mile and a half from reasonable protection, and unable to cooperate with Major Powell is of constant annoyance to officers in command of guards, who endeavor to give all the protection in their power. Gen'l Smith will remember the trouble we had on this point during our late march En route to join this Post with Contract trains.

I take great pleasure in mentioning the zeal and efficiency of the Officers, Lieutenants Connolly, Paulus and McCarthy, and the men of my Command.

Having covered I think, all the ground concerning my movements,

I have the honor to be
Very Respectfully
Your Ob't Servant
(signed) B.E. Smith
Major 27th Inf.
Bvt Lt. Col. U.S. A.

To Lieut. A.H. Bowman
27th U.S. Infantry Post Adj

*   *   *

Head Quarters Company "C" 27th Infantry
Fort Phil Kearny D.T. August 4, 1867
To The Post Adjutant,
Fort Philip Kearny D.T.:

Sir:

I have the honor to present for the information of the Post and Department Commanders, a report of the engagement between a large body of hostile Indians, supposed to be Sioux Cheyennes and Arappahoes [sic], numbering at the lowest estimate three thousand (3000) men, and part of my Company © 27th Infantry) consisting of twenty-six enlisted [men], four citizens and two officers (myself included), which occurred near Piney Island, five miles from this post on the 2d day of August 1867.

On the 31st day of July 1867 pursuant to Special Order No. 128, bearing date July 31st 1867, I left this post with fifty-one (51) enlisted men and one (1) officer, for the purpose of escorting and furnishing details to protect the laboring parties engaged by contractor J. R. Porter in hauling fuel to the post. Upon my arrival at the above named place I found the train divided; one part encamped on a plateau, and with one exception, the position well selected for defense, and the best security the country afforded for the stock: the other part was encamped about one mile distant in a south westerly [sic] direction on a commanding point across the Little Piney Creek, at the foot of the mountains. My details consisted in sending twelve (12) men to protect the working parties of both trains and thirteen (13) men as escort to the trains when coming into the post.

On the morning in question I had made the usual details, which left the twenty six [sic] men, four (4) citizens and one (1) oficer [sic] above mentioned at my disposal.

About 9 o'clock in the morning two hundred (200) Indians attacked the herders in charge of the herd, driving them off; at the same time some five hundred (500) attacked the train at the foot of the mountains, driving off the men belonging there and burning it. Some fifteen minutes afterwards I was surrounded by about eight hundred (800) mounted Indians, but owing to the very effective fire of my small party they were driven back with considerable loss. Finding they could not enter the corral they retired to a hill about six hundred (600) yards distant and there stripped for more determined fighting: then with additional reinforcements continued to charge us on foot for three consecutive hours, but were each time repulsed.

The hills in the immediate vicinity were covered with Indians who merely acted as spectators, until they saw how fruitles [sic] were the efforts of their comrades near my corral when they also moved up, and seemed determined to carry my position at all hazards and massacre my command, which they would undoubtedly have done but that Bvt. Lieut. Col. Benjamin F. Smith, Major 27th U.S. Inft. Was seen approaching with reinforcements, when they retired, leaving some of their dead and wounded near the corral, thus closing the fight about half past twelve (12) o'clock P.M.

In my opinion there were not less than sixty (60) Indians killed on the spot, and one hundred and twenty (120) severely wounded, although the citizens who took part in the action are of the opinion that my estimate is far below the actual figures.

The following is a list of the casualties at my corral.

Killed

1 Lieutenant John C. Jenness 27th U.S. Infantry
Private   Thomas C. Doyle   "   "   "
"   Henry Haggerty   "   "   "
"   Horace Kittridge   Killed while escaping from the other corral
"   Hermana Song   "   "   "   "   "   "   "   "
"   George W. Haines   "   "   "   "   "   "   "   "

Wounded

Private   Nelson V. Deming Co. C 27th Inft, shoulder
"   John L. Somers   "   "   "   " thigh

That we escaped with such a comparatively small loss considering the large number operating against us, and their being so well provided with carbines and other breach [sic] loading arms, is due in a very great measure to the gallantry and coolness displayed by the men of my command together with their excellent marksmanship. In the death of Lieutenant Jenness the service has lost a gallant and promising young officer, one who had endeared himself to his comrades and who on the morning of his death fell while setting a noble example of coolness and daring to those who were serving with him.

I am Sir
Very respectfully
Your obedient servant

(signed) James Powell
Captain Co "C" 27th Infantry
Brevet Major U S A
Commanding Company

Official:
(signed) A.H. Bowman
1 Lieutenant 27th Infantry
Post Adjutant

Recollections of the Wagon Box Fight

by Samuel Gibson, Max Littman, and Frederic Claus*

Author's Preface

The following recollections of the Wagon Box Fight provide three first person accounts by participants in that event and as such are a valuable primary source of information. Notwithstanding, it should be borne in mind that these recollections were given many years later when memories were subject to the normal distortion of advancing years. As a consequence, the accounts are not in complete agreement, as, for example, Gibson's description of the mounted charges, as opposed to Littman's recollection that all charges were on foot. It should also be pointed out that Gibson's reference to Powell's estimate of Indian casualties is misleading. Powell, in his official report, estimated 60 killed and 120 wounded. Also, Max Littman is in error when he states that the Indians had never encountered breech-loading rifles prior to the Wagon Box Fight.

Finally, it is regrettable that we do not have similar eye-witness accounts of the fight from the Indian viewpoint.

* From *The Bozeman Trail*, by Grace Raymond Hebard and E. A. Brininstool (1922)

The Wagon Box Fight
by Samuel Gibson
Twenty-seventh U. S. Infantry

I had been a member of Carrington's expedition from Fort Kearney, Nebraska, in May, 1866, and was at Fort Phil Kearney (then situated in the territory of Dakota, which included the present state of Wyoming) from the time of its erection until the post was ordered abandoned by the government early in the fall of 1868. After the arrival of General Wessels, the winter continued one of unusual severity, with the thermometer down to twenty-five and forty degrees below zero most of the time. We had no fresh meat, no vegetables. We did get one small loaf of bread issued to us daily; just about enough for one meal, and after that was gone we had to fall back on musty hardtack, salt pork and black coffee. Occasionally we had bean soup. We had no place in barracks to wash, and after the creeks were frozen over we could not take a bath until they thawed out the following spring.

The Indians did not bother us at all the balance of the early part of the winter of 1867, although we were in mortal terror that they would try some new deviltry every day that we were in the pinery, getting out logs, as it was necessary to do this to furnish firewood to cook our rations and warm our barracks.

Colonel Carrington and his family, with Mrs. Grummond, the widow of Lieutenant Grummond, who had been killed in the Fetterman fight, together with the Eighteenth Infantry band, left the post the latter part of January, 1867, for Fort Caspar, leaving General Wessels in command at Fort Phil Kearney. He had nineteen sentries posted on and around the stockade every day and night, there being three reliefs of the guard. Fifty-nine men mounted guard every day, besides the officer of the day and four non-commissioned officers. This large detail of men for guard duty worked great hardship on us, for in addition, we had to saw wood for our stoves in quarters. Then, many of our comrades were sick with scurvy, and the hospital was filled with invalids, many of whom died.

As soon as spring opened, the bull trains commenced to come up from Fort Laramie, and with them came Red Cloud and his red devils, the Sioux, again. They immediately began their tactics of the previous summer, attacking every train that passed over the Bozeman Trail, and harrying our wood trains every day or so.

During June, Gilmore & Porter's bull train arrived at the fort with wagons loaded with rations, forage, etc. We were mighty pleased to see them, but what tickled us most was the seven hundred new breech-loading Springfield rifles of fifty-caliber, with one hundred thousand rounds of ammunition, which they brought to supersede the old muzzle-loaders with which we had been previously armed.

Gilmore & Porter remained at the post all summer. They had taken a contract from our quartermaster, General George P. Dandy [sic: Quartermaster, Captain George B. Dandy], to supply the fort with logs for the sawmills, and firewood for the following winter. In order to protect their stock from night attacks by Indians, the contractors improvised a corral six miles west of the fort on a level plain. They removed the boxes from their wagons, fourteen in number, and formed them into an oval shaped enclosure into which their stock was driven every night. The pinery where the logs were being cut was at some little distance from the wagon box corral. Several tents were pitched just outside the corral where the woodchoppers and soldiers bunked. Seven thousand rounds of ammunition were arranged inside the corral, and everybody was instructed, in case of an Indian attack at the pinery, to retreat to the corral, where it was considered that a good defense could be made until relief arrived from the fort.

It was early in July when the contractors formed the corral, and Company A of my regiment, the Twenty-seventh Infantry, was sent out with the train, as a guard for the month, to do escort duty to and from the fort daily, and also to protect the woodchoppers in the pinery. Company A saw Indians but two or three times during the entire month of July. On July 31st, Company C, to which I belonged, relieved Company A. Packing our wagons with a month's rations we marched out from Fort Phil Kearney, across Sullivant Hills, to the woodchoppers' camp near the lower pinery.

We pitched our tents around the outside of the corral. There were spaces between the wagon beds wide enough for a man to walk through, but not large enough for a steer to push outside. There were two of the wagon beds which had canvas covers on them—one at the extreme east end, holding the rations of the woodchoppers, and one on the south side which held our company rations and miscellaneous stores. There was also a wagon complete, with extra rations for the woodchoppers standing outside the corral at the west end, which contained the bedding of the woodchoppers. This wagon stood some ten feet from the wagon boxes which formed the corral. It had a canvas cover over the bows.

On August 1st I was with the detail guarding the woodchoppers at the lower pinery, and was on picket all day. Several of us, when questioned by the sergeant in charge of the detail as to whether we had seen any Indians, replied that we had not, but that we "thought we could smell them." The sergeant, McQuiery, gave us an incredulous look and gruffly exclaimed, "Smell hell" with extreme contempt.

That night we, who had been on picket duty all day, formed the guard around the camp. Two sentinels were posted, one at the east end and one at the west end of the corral, with strict orders from Captain Powell to allow no one to enter the camp, and to challenge anyone or anything approaching; also, if there was the slightest suspicion in our minds, to open fire upon the approaching objects, or upon anything that looked like Indians.

The night was clear and starry above us, but toward the mountains and down the Big Piney valley it looked awfully dark and ominous. Private Jack McDonough's dog, "Jess," was around with the sentinels all night, and although we could not see or hear anything suspicious, the animal would run furiously down the hill toward the Big Piney valley every few minutes, barking and snapping furiously.

I have always since believed that Red Cloud's warriors were in the valley and around our camp all that night of August 1st, waiting for a chance to surprise us during the night or at day-break, when we were supposed to be somewhat off our guard.

At day-break on August 2d, the cooks were called early to get up and prepare breakfast for the company. A detail of pickets was sent to the point on the banks of the Little Piney between the two camps. Our drummer-boy, Hines, beat the reveille first call, and fifteen minutes later the company fell in, and answered revielle [sic] roll call—some, alas, for the last time.

Breakfast was announced by Cook Brown calling "Chuck" and immediately after, the company broke ranks and laid away their rifles. The whole company took breakfast, with the exception of two men still on picket around the corral. By this time the sun had risen, and we scanned the horizon and the foothills to the north and down the valley of the Big Piney.

We could not see the least sign of an Indian, although we learned afterward that they were watching our every movement from points of vantage in the hills. I was told this some years later by Chief Rain-in-the-Face while I was a sergeant of Company H, Twenty-second Infantry, at Standing Rock agency, during the Sioux Ghost Dance war of 1890-1891.

Immediately after breakfast the wagon trains started for their different destinations—one going to the fort loaded with logs which had been brought out of the pinery the day before, with a detachment of twenty men, commanded by Lieutenant Francis McCarthy and Corporal Paddy Conley, who accompanied the train as an escort. If my memory serves me right, Mr. Porter who owned the bull train and had the contract for supplying the wood to the quartermaster at Fort Phil Kearney, went along.

The other train pulled out for the lower pinery with an escort of thirteen men. Jack McDonough, Dave Moore, McNally and McCumber are the names of some of this escort, which was commanded by Corporal Riley Porter. With Porter was "Portugee" Phillips, who had carried the dispatches of Colonel Carrington from Fort Phil Kearney to Horseshoe Station after the Fetterman disaster of December 21, the previous year. Phillips was accompanied by a man named Judd. Both Phillips and Judd had sub-contracts from Mr. Porter, the contractor.

About this time, 6:45, a.m., I was ordered by the first sergeant to proceed, fully armed and equipped, and relieve Private John Grady as lance corporal in charge of the picket-post on the banks of the Little Piney. Having relieved Grady, who instructed me to keep a sharp lookout for Indians, I fixed up a sort of shade from the hot sun with willows stuck in the ground and ponchos tied over the tops. I had laid under this canopy for perhaps fifteen minutes with a private named Deming, when suddenly Guard Garrett yelled "Indians."

Deming and I jumped to our feet, and sure enough, away to the west of us we counted seven Indians, mounted, coming across the divide from the north on a dead run and in single file, riding toward the Little Piney and chanting their war song. As the Indians were coming in an oblique direction toward us, and as not a man in the company had yet fired a shot at an Indian from the new breech-loading fifty-caliber Springfield rifles with which we had just been armed, I sat down and adjusted my sights to seven hundred yards, and laying my rifle on top of a stone breastwork, took steady aim at the Indian in advance and fired. My bullet struck a stone in front of the Indian, ricocheted off and wounded his pony. The Indian was thrown off, but immediately sprang to his feet as his pony fell, and was taken up behind a mounted warrior who was following closely in his rear.

About this time Deming and I looked toward our main camp, and over the Big Piney, to the foothills toward the north, and there we saw more Indians than we had ever seen before. Deming exclaimed in an excited tone: "Look at the Indians!" and pointing toward the foothills across Big Piney Creek, he added: "My God! there are thousands of them."

Hearing shots across the Little Piney, I ordered Garrett to watch for signals from the main camp, and sent Deming across the Little Piney to see what was going on at the other camp, which was a woodchoppers' camp consisting of seven or eight wagons. This camp was perhaps twelve hundred yards directly south of our main camp. Garrett and I watched the Indians coming across the foothills, like a big swarm of bees, on the north side of the Big Piney, feeling very uneasy the while about our failure to receive any signals to return to the main camp where the wagon boxes were corralled [*sic*]. Deming soon came back and reported that Indians had run off the herd, and that all the men, including four of our soldiers (Harris, Kittredge, Lang and Kilberg), who were guarding the small camp south of Little Piney, had run for the mountains, and that one of the civilians, a herder, was coming across the creek, leading his pony, to join us.

Looking toward the main camp we saw quite a commotion going on. The men were hurrying here and there. By this time the herder had come across the creek and joined us, and I told Deming and Garrett that we would start at once for the main camp, and that if the Indians got after us we would make a running skirmish for it. The plan was that we would stop alternately and fire two or three shots, following each other up closely, with myself in the rear.

We immediately started on a good brisk walk, but had retreated only about seventy-five or a hundred yards before the Indians commenced coming up out of the Little Piney Creek bottom by ones, twos and threes at different places. The first one I saw was coming up the bank of the creek sideways, and he carried an old Spencer carbine which he was waving excitedly. I immediately "pulled down" on him just as he was aiming at me. My bullet knocked him off his 'pony, and I heard his shot whizz [*sic*] past my head.

By this time Garrett had stopped and was down on one knee, firing at the Indians who had come up out of the creek higher up to the west of us. I ran past Garrett toward camp, and saw Deming on my right, shooting at the Indians. At this moment the citizen herder, who was leading his pony by the bridle-rein, told me to stick my bayonet in the animal's flanks to make him go faster. I told him to turn the pony loose and shoot at the Indians, who had by this time increased in numbers at such an alarming rate that they seemed to rise out of the ground like a flock of birds. All of them were naked, with the exception of the regulation "gee-string" around their waists, while some of them wore gorgeous war-bonnets; others had a single feather in their scalp-locks. Their bodies were painted white, green and yellow, which made them look hideous in the extreme.

All of us were now on the dead run. Even the herder's pony was clipping it off, with half a dozen arrows sticking in his flanks, and it seemed as if hell had broken loose. The Indians whooped and yelled as they rode hither and thither and backward and forward in their efforts to surround us by circling, endeavoring thereby to cut us off from the main camp. Each one of us knew full well that if we were hit by an arrow or bullet it would mean death—or something worse if captured alive. We realized that if disabled our scalps would soon be dangling at the scalp-pole of some Sioux warrior. We had seen and assisted in collecting the bodies of our comrades who were so horribly mutilated at the Fetterman fight, and knew that a similar fate awaited us if we were cut off. We kept on running and shooting, expecting every minute to feel a bullet or an arrow in our backs.

We soon saw one of our men run out to meet us from the main camp. He dropped on one knee about a hundred yards from the main corral and opened a rapid fire on the advancing hordes of savages. Several fell from their ponies under his accurate fire. This man proved to be one of our sergeants, Littman by name, who, by his courage and thoughtfulness in coming out to meet us, and the rapidity and effectiveness of his fire, saved us from being surrounded and cut off by the red devils. We were thus enabled to reach the main camp in the wagon box corral, although we were in a completely exhausted condition. The civilian herder who was leading his pony, was the last one to enter the corral.

Upon our arrival, completely winded from our long and dangerous run, I immediately reported to Captain Powell, who was standing outside and on the south side of the corral, where he had evidently observed our retreat and pursuit by the Indians. To him, in a panting and exhausted condition, I reported why we had left the picket-post without orders, as it was impossible for us to hold it against such overwhelming odds.

Looking me straight in the eye, Captain Powell exclaimed: "You have done nobly, my boy! You could not have done better." Then addressing the three of us) he said "Men, find a place in the wagon boxes. You'll have to fight for your lives today."

We saluted and turned to obey his orders, at the same time following his instructions to provide ourselves with plenty of ammunition.

To my dying day I shall never forget the fierce "do-or-die" look on Captain Powell's face that morning. Deming, Garrett and I split up, and each man carried into his wagon box plenty of loaded shells. The Indians were not aware that we had received new rifles, and supposed that after we had fired one shot they would be able to ride us down before we could reload.

Much has been said by historians and others who have written short accounts of this fight, regarding the wagon boxes inside of which we fought. Some have said that the boxes were made of boiler-iron, and others that they were lined with steel and had loopholes through the sides. All such statements are absolutely without foundation. They were the ordinary government wagon boxes, part of the same equipment used during the Civil War. They were built simply of thin wood, while some of them were make-shift wagons belonging to the contractor's bull train; the heaviest of them being made of but one inch boards. There was not a particle of iron about them anywhere, except the bolts, stay-straps and nuts used in holding the rickety concerns together. I also have read in some accounts that the wagon boxes were "a kind of traveling fort supplied by the government." Any statement that the wagon boxes used as protection in this fight of August 2, 1867, were other than plain, ordinary wood wagon boxes, is a fabrication pure and simple, no matter on what authority given.

I soon found a place in one of the wagon beds on the south side of the corral, and here I found Sergeant McQuiery and Private John Grady. Grady was the only one to speak to me, inviting me to come in with them, saying: "You'll have to fight like hell today, kid, if you expect to get out of this alive." I was the youngest boy in the company, being but eighteen years of age, and was always called "the kid," which appellation was given me by Dan Flynn, a member of Company H.

Leaning my rifle against the sides of the wagon beds, I carried a hundred rounds of ammunition to my place, and then took a walk around among the men who were standing in groups inside and outside of the corral watching the Indians assembling all around us. I spoke to some of the men, but no one answered me, and the expression of their faces will haunt me as long as I live. I had been in a score of fights and skirmishes with most of my comrades since we began to build Fort Phil Kearney in July of 1866, and had been with some of these same men when we went out with Colonel Carrington on December 22d of that fatal year to bring in the remainder of Fetterman's command from Massacre Hill, where they were killed the previous day, and had then seen the stern, revengeful looks on their faces; but the looks in their eyes this morning was altogether different. It was a look, not of despair or desperation, but one of intense earnestness and resolution.

I saw Private Tommy Doyle piling up some neck-yokes belonging to the bull train on top of one another for the purpose of forming a breastwork, between the ends of two of the wagon boxes. I saw another man, Sergeant Frank Robertson, an old soldier who had served in the old Seventh and Tenth Infantry, taking the shoestrings out of his shoes and tying them together, with a loop at one end, which he fitted over his right foot, and a smaller loop at the other end to fit over the trigger of his rifle. I did not ask him what he was doing, because the awful horror of our isolated position seemed to dawn upon my mind, but I knew too well the meaning of those grim preparations-that the red devils would never get old Frank Robertson alive!

I then joined a group of five or six men outside the corral at the southwest end, and in the midst of them stood Lieutenant John C. Jenness, who was watching the Indians through a field glass down the Big Piney valley to the north, and on the highest point of the hill on the ridge east of us. There seemed to be hundreds of Indians, all mounted on their finest and handsomest war ponies, riding here and there, chanting their war and death songs. In the valley, more were assembling. Lieutenant Jenness seemed to be watching the big bunch of Indians on the high hill about three-quarters of a mile distant, and I heard him say to Captain Powell, who soon, joined us: "Captain, I believe that Red Cloud is on top of that hill," (pointing to the east). The captain made no reply, but hearing a commotion, accompanied by loud talking, among the men to the south of us, he turned, and seeing the Indians riding furiously about on the plains between Little Piney and Big Piney Creeks, he exclaimed:

"Men here they come! Take your places and shoot to kill!"

And those were the only words of command given by him, save once, during the entire fight.

Each man quickly took his place in the wagon boxes. Not a word was spoken by anyone, and the silence was awful. When I took my place in the wagon box occupied by Sergeant McQuiery and Private John Grady, both of them had their shoes off, and were fixing their shoestrings into loops to fit over the right foot and from thence to the trigger of their rifles, for the same purpose that Sergeant Robertson had done—to kill themselves when all hope was lost, in the event the Indians passed over our barricade by an overwhelming force of numbers, when every man would stand erect, place the muzzle of his loaded rifle under his chin and take his own life, rather than be captured and made to endure the inevitable torture. I had just taken off my own shoes and made loops in the strings when the firing began.

Resting my rifle on the top of the wagon box I began firing with the rest. The whole plain was alive with Indians, all mounted and visible in every direction. They were riding madly about, and shooting at us with guns, bows and arrows, first on one side and then on the other of the corral. Then they would circle, and each time come in closer, uttering the most piercing and unearthly war cries. Some of the more venturesome would ride in close and throw spears at us. Others would brandish their war-clubs and tomahawks at us, and others, still more daring, would ride within a hundred yards, then suddenly drop on the off side of their ponies, and all we could see would be an arm or a leg sticking above the pony's back, and "whizz"[sic] would come the arrows! They paid dearly for their daring, for we had a steady rest for our rifles, the Indians were all within easy point-blank range, and we simply mowed them down by scores.

The tops of the wagon beds were literally ripped and torn to slivers by their bullets. How we ever escaped with such a slight loss I never have been able to understand. After we had commenced firing, a great number of Indians rode in very close—probably within a hundred and fifty yards, and sitting on their ponies waited for us to draw ramrods for reloading, as they supposed we were yet using the old muzzle-loaders, but, thanks to God and Lieutenant-General Sherman, the latter had listened to the appeals of Colonel Carrington, commanding Fort Phil Kearney the previous year, and we had just been armed with the new weapon, and instead of drawing ramrods and thus losing precious time, we simply threw open the breech-blocks of our new rifles to eject the empty, shell and slapped in fresh ones. This puzzled the Indians, and they were soon glad to withdraw to a safe distance.

The plain in front of us was strewn with dead and dying Indians and ponies. The Indians were amazed, but not by any means undaunted. They were there for blood, and came in such hordes that they were ready for any sacrifice if they could but capture our little party. They made heroic attempts to recover their wounded. It was their lives or ours. We had not forgotten Massacre Hill. We were not fiends, gloating over the suffering of their wounded, but that bloody day of December 21st was fresh in our minds, and we were filled with a grim determination to kill, just as we had seen our comrades killed. There was no thought of wavering. We knew from their countless numbers that if they overwhelmed us they could easily capture the fort, but six miles distant, where there were helpless women and children. We were fighting for their lives as well as our own. It was not revenge but retribution.

After recovering a great number of their dead and wounded at a fearful sacrifice of life, the Indians withdrew to a safe distance, but while recovering their injured we witnessed the most magnificent display of horsemanship imaginable. Two mounted Indians would ride like the wind among the dead and wounded, and seeing an arm or leg thrust upward, would ride one on each side of the wounded savage, reach over and pick him up on the run, and carry him to a place of safety. This was done many times, and we could not help but admire their courage and daring.

During the lull in the firing, we got a fresh supply of cartridges out of the seven cases holding a thousand rounds each, which had been opened by order of Captain Powell some time before the firing started, and had been placed about the corral at convenient places. We had to crawl on our hands and knees to get the ammunition, and I saw several of the men, crawling like myself, to get cartridges. None of them spoke a word to me, and the utter silence was uncanny.

When I got back to my wagon bed I heard some man in the box next to me ask in a loud whisper for a chew of tobacco. While I had been getting my ammunition I asked a man named Phillips, who was also getting shells if anyone had been shot. He shook his head and simply whispered, "Don't know." After I got back to my place I looked around and saw Captain Powell, who was in the second box west of me, with Sergeant Frank Hoover, and both of them were firing at some wounded Indians within sixty yards of the corral to the west.

Lieutenant John C. Jenness was leaning over the cover of the wagon bed at the west end of the corral, firing at some Indians on the northwest side, where they lay partially concealed under the brow of the hill where the land sloped down toward Big Piney valley. On the north side of the corral, in a very irregular form, the land on which we were encamped came to an abrupt termination, sloping down toward the Big Piney Valley. The nearest point from the corral was probably seventy-five yards northwest, and extended a greater distance toward the east. It was behind this ridge where the Indians on foot had placed themselves in scores, all armed with rifles, and all one could see of them would be the two sticks across which they rested their guns. When they raised their heads to take aim we could see the single feather sticking up in their scalp-locks. It was these Indians who killed Lieutenant Jenness and Privates Doyle and Haggerty.

While watching Lieutenant Jenness I heard Sergeant McQuirey ask in a hoarse whisper if anyone had been killed or wounded. I answered that I did not know. The Indians, both mounted and on foot, were still trying to rescue their dead and wounded from the plain in front of us; and on the plain to the southeast a large body of Indians were signaling with pocket-mirrors toward the big ridge east of us, while couriers were observed riding furiously back and forth at break-neck speed, going and coming by way of Big Piney valley. We did not know what to expect, but we knew they would attack us again soon. Something desperate had evidently been determined upon by the savages. All we could do was to wait and watch. Not a word was spoken. It was a moment of suspense that was simply terrible.

As we sat and waited for what we thought would be the finish of us, I looked along the wagon beds and saw my comrades sitting there watching the assembling of the Indians. Every man had his jaws firmly closed, with a grim determination to fight until we were over-powered. We did not know what time it was and nobody cared.

The fight had commenced about seven o'clock in the morning, and I did not hear any man ask about the time of day during the fight. Nearly all of us were bareheaded, as we had used our caps and hats to hold ammunition. The sun beat down with a pitiless glare that terrible August day, and it seemed like eternity to us all.

Suddenly someone on the north side of the corral yelled, "Look out! they're coming again!" We could see the Indians to the east, south and southwest of us galloping about and circling toward us, coming nearer and nearer. All at once some soldier shouted in a loud voice: "The tents!"

The line of tents were in front of us on the south side and had been left standing all the time of the first fierce charge, and we had simply fired through the spaces between them. No one had thought of pulling them down until that moment. Then two men leaped out of a wagon bed to the east of us, ran toward the tents but a short distance away, and began pulling them to the ground.

At this moment Private John Grady, who sat near me in my wagon bed, yelled: "Come on, kid!" As he leaped over the wagon bed I followed him, with the bullets zipping about us and the arrows swishing past and striking into the ground on all sides of us. We loosened the loops around the tent-pins at the corners, working together, until all but the last of the tents dropped; and as Grady and I started toward the last one—an officers' tent, sixty or seventy feet in front of ours, to the south, we heard Sergeant Hoover shout: "Come back here! you'll get hit! Never mind the captain's tent! Get into your wagon box and shoot!" We dropped everything, and amid a perfect hail of balls and arrows rushed back and leaped over into our wagon beds again. How we escaped has been the mystery of my life, but neither of us were even hit.

With the tents down, we could see the Indians to much better advantage, and were enabled to deliver a more effective fire. The whole plain was again alive with countless swarms of the warriors, assembling for another grand charge upon us. Our fire was terribly destructive and deadly in accuracy, and we repulsed them again, but our gun-barrels were so overheated from the rapidity of our fire that the metal burned our hands, and we were obliged to open the breech-blocks during this lull to allow the barrels to cool off. During one of these momentary lulls Grady asked me to go after more ammunition. I crawled out of the wagon box westward, and saw several other men after more ammunition, and as I looked toward the west end I saw the body of Lieutenant Jenness lying where he had fallen, shot through the head and heart. Within a few feet of the corpse, Private Jim Condon was fighting behind a barrel of beans placed in the interval between Captain Powell's wagon bed and the one with a cover on.

Having secured the ammunition, I crawled back in my wagon bed. Here I told Sergeant McQuiery and Private Grady that Lieutenant Jenness had been killed, and of the manner in which he had apparently been shot. They both exclaimed: "Good God! Anyone else?" I answered that I did not know, and as the Indians were still making false charges toward us to recover their dead and wounded, we opened a desultory fire upon them.

About this time word was passed around that Privates Henry Haggerty and Tommy Doyle had been killed on the north side of the corral. The brave little Jerseyman, Haggerty, had been shot through the left shoulder earlier in the fight, but the fact had been kept secret by the other men in the same wagon bed, lest some men become disheartened. The men in the box with Haggerty wanted him to lie down after getting shot through the shoulder, but with his left arm hanging useless at his side, he had used his good right, and kept on loading and firing for over two hours, until the Indians on the north ridge finally killed him by sending a bullet through the top of his head. Doyle had been killed some time after the first charge, while bravely fighting behind a breastwork of ox-yokes. He was struck in the forehead.

It was now becoming a question of water. Men were everywhere asking for it, and the supply was getting woefully scarce, and the suffering from the terrific beat and nervous strain was intense. Added to this, the Indians had rained fire-arrows inside the corral, which set fire to the dry manure within the enclosure, and the stench from this was abominable. I had filled my canteen in Little Piney Creek that morning and had brought it back to the corral on the retreat from the picket-post, so that we three in my wagon box had all the water we desired up to that time, and there was still some left. Grady took up the canteen and drank a mouthful, but immediately spat it out again, exclaiming that it was too hot for him. Sergeant McQuiery then washed out his mouth with some, remarking: "It IS pretty warm, but water is too precious to waste just now." Soon after this Sergeant Robertson started crawling on his hands and knees, coming from the east end of the corral toward the west end, poking aside with his head the arrows that were sticking up in the ground. When he arrived at the place where the body of Lieutenant Jenness was lying, he placed a wagon cover over it, and then returned to his wagon bed at the east end of the corral.

There was a barrel half full of water standing outside the corral at the west end when the fighting began. It was about twenty feet away from the wagon beds. During the fighting it had been struck by bullets and the water had nearly all leaked out. Under the covered wagon, close to the west end of the corral. were two camp kettles in which our coffee had been made for breakfast, and Brown, the cook, had filled them with water on top of the old coffee grounds, intending to use the coffee for the company supper. Private Jim Condon had seen the water leaking from the barrel, and had passed the word around the corral that the barrel was empty, or nearly so. Then Cook Brown volunteered the information that the camp kettles had been filled with water, and as they were but a short distance away, we immediately planned to secure them.

My comrade, Johnny Grady, who sat next to me in our wagon bed, was crazy for water. He said: "Kid, let's go and get one of those kettles." I replied, "All right." We took a careful look about and then commenced crawling on our stomachs through the arrows that lined the corral, and as we reached the wagon bed with the cover on at the west end, Jim Condon, from behind the barrel of beans where he was fighting, cautioned us to be on the lookout or the Indians would get us sure.

The men on the north side seemed to divine our purpose, and word was passed along to keep up a steady fire on the Indians along the ridge. We crawled through the opening between the wagon beds, hugging the ground as closely as possible, and soon reached the place where the kettles stood without having apparently been detected. We each grabbed a kettle and then commenced crawling back, pulling the kettles along. We had gotten about half-way to safety, when "bang! bang! bang!" came several shots from the Indians to the north of us, and "zzip! p-i-n-g-g-g!" we heard some of the bullets strike the kettles, but, fortunately without injuring us. We both thought our time had come, but we finally got back inside the corral with those kettles of dirty black water. When I looked at mine, there were two holes clean through it, and consequently I had lost some of the water, but we left them both with Private Condon, who gave each man a good drink when he crawled out of his wagon box for it.

The time between each charge dragged heavily, and the day seemed almost endless. Yet, the Indians on the north side of us, hidden under the ridge, kept us constantly on the alert, and some of them at the east end of the ridge, about two hundred yards from the east side of the corral, would run out toward us once in a while, armed with spears and tomahawks, each carrying a big shield made of buffalo-hide. There they would brandish their weapons in a menacing manner and utter shrill war cries. There was one big giant of an Indian who had thus run out several times from the ridge to the east, and he always managed to escape our fire, until he apparently thought he bore a charmed life, and that we could not kill him. He was truly a magnificent specimen of Indian manhood, nearly seven feet tall and almost wholly naked. He had led all of the previous charges from the east end of the ridge, and must have been a sub-chief. The last time he appeared must have been about two o'clock in the afternoon, and this time he came out slowly but grandly, with his big buffalo shield in front of him, brandishing his spear and chanting a war-song. Then he would hold his shield on one side and run toward us, jumping into the air and alternating this movement by dodging to one side. The sight was fascinating, and we could not but admire his superb courage. Several of us had fired at him but without effect, when one of the boys at the east end remarked: "We have simply got to get that fellow, as he thinks we can't hit him." We carefully adjusted our sights, taking accurate aim, and just as he shifted his shield aside and began running toward us, we fired together, and he leaped into the air and came down as limp as a rag, fairly riddled with bullets. We all breathed easier after this warrior was killed, for his death seemed to put a stop to any more charges from that direction.

The Indians had withdrawn out of range, except those concealed under the brow of the ridge on the north side. These would take a shot at us every few minutes. The main body of Indians was around the big hill at the end of the ridge east of us, where Red Cloud was stationed in supreme command, and we could plainly hear him or some other chief haranguing them in a loud voice. Presently a great number of Indians rode down the Big Piney valley out of sight. Another party, several hundred in number, rode out on the plain toward us, evidently for another charge. We all knew that they had lost scores of their braves in killed and wounded, and in their maddened frenzy would make another attempt to overwhelm us by force of superior numbers, and would take horrible revenge upon us if they captured us.

It must have been after three o'clock in the afternoon when, straining our eyes for the sight of that line of skirmishers in the glorious blue uniform (which appeared later) we could distinctly hear a sort of humming sound, seemingly made by many voices, below us in the Big Piney valley. Some of us thought it was the squaws wailing over their dead warriors, and as the sound grew louder some of the men on the north side of the corral rose to their feet to see if they could discern anything below them in the Big Piney valley, but they had no sooner risen to their feet than others yelled at them, "Down, down, or you will get hit!"

As we waited in silent wonderment at this strange sound, unlike anything we had ever heard before, the echo appeared to come from the northwest of the corral. The Indians to the east and south of us had come out on the plain, where they were circling and coming nearer all the time, brandishing their spears and war clubs at us and giving voice to their war cries. Those of the warriors who were armed with guns immediately opened fire again upon us, and we at once replied, killing and wounding many more of them. During this time, that awful humming, chanting sound grew in volume and intensity, coming nearer and nearer, now directly from west of us. The Indians to the south had withdrawn out of range, and seemed to be waiting for something to happen.

And something DID happen I Suddenly there was a cry from the west end of the corral: "Here they come!" We all looked in that direction, and saw a sight which none of those yet alive will ever forget to their dying day. It chilled my blood at the time. We saw the naked bodies of hundreds upon hundreds of Indians swarming up a ravine about ninety yards to the west of the corral. They were all on foot, formed in the shape of a letter V, or wedge, and were led by Red Cloud's nephew, who wore a gorgeous war bonnet. Immediately we opened a terrific fire upon them, under which nothing could stand, and at the very first volley Red Cloud's nephew fell, pierced by many bullets. Nothing daunted, the forces came on slowly, and in great numbers, the places of those who fell under our fire being taken immediately by others.

So close were the Indian hordes by this time that the heavy rifle bullets from our guns must have gone through two or three bodies. They were so near us that we could even see the whites of their eyes. As they swarmed toward us with shrill cries and piercing whoops, Private Jim Condon jumped to his feet from behind his barrel of beans, and shouted, as he waved his rifle over his head: "Come on, you blathering sons av guns! We kin lick th' hull damn bunch av yez!" Captain Powell, who was close by Condon, at once ordered him to lie down. And now the Indians were so close that it seemed as if nothing could prevent their swarming over our barricade and into the corral, when it would have been all over with us in no time. Our fire was accurate, coolly delivered and given with most telling effect, but nevertheless it looked for a minute as though our last moment on earth had come. just when it seemed as if all hope was gone, the Indians suddenly broke and fled. They could not stand before the withering fire we poured into their ranks. The several hundred mounted Indians, on the plain to the south of us, who were intently watching this foot-charge, never offered to assist their red brothers by making a mounted charge, but discreetly remained out of rifle range. During all these charges against our corral, Red Cloud who was in supreme command, stood (or sat on his horse) on top of the ridge due east of our little improvised fort. Some of the boys estimated it to be three-quarters of a mile away. After this last charge of the Indians on foot from the west, and while we were waiting to see what the red devils would try next, some six or eight of us elevated the sights on our rifles to the full extension of long range firing, and let loose five or six volleys at Red Cloud and his crowd on top of the hill and we all fully believed, from the sudden scattering of Indians, that some of our bullets found lodgment and made "good Injuns" of some of them. Suddenly the Indians on the big hill at the top of the ridge started down the steep decline into Big Piney valley by twos, threes and fours. We took a few long range shots at them, which served to accelerate their speed very effectively. We did not understand this maneuver for a few minutes.

Just then someone at the east end of the corral cried out: "Hark! did you hear that?" Everybody ceased firing, and in another moment we distinctly heard the boom of a big gun to the east of us. It was indeed heavenly music to all of us. It was the sorely needed relief from Fort Phil Kearney. They had heard the sounds of battle and started reinforcements, with a howitzer, to our succor. It was this big gun that was driving the savages off the big hill. The Indians on the plain south of us could also be seen disappearing into the pinery to the west. We knew what the commotion meant, but waited, with nerves and senses wrought almost to a frenzy. Suddenly one of the men jumped to his feet, shouting: "Here they come, boys! Hurrah!" and as we looked toward the east we could see those glorious old McClelland caps on the heads of our comrades as they appeared in a long skirmish line.

Then we all jumped to our feet and yelled. We threw our caps in the air. We hugged each other in the ecstacy of our joy. We laughed, cried and fairly sobbed like little children in the delirium of our delight. The awful strain was over.

Captain Powell suddenly ordered everybody back into the wagon beds, lest another charge be made by the Indians before our rescuers should reach us. We obediently returned to our places, and sat watching the skirmish line advancing, while the boom of the big gun was the sweetest sound that ever fell on our ears.

The gunners were throwing shells into a big bunch of Indians in the Big Piney valley.

The redskins began scattering rapidly across Big Piney Creek and were soon out of range. The skirmish line continued to advance, and in a few minutes we saw the main body marching in front of a small wagon train of ten or twelve six-mule teams of empty ambulances and wagons, with the big brass cannon in front of the teams.

By this time everybody was talking and waving their arms as we recognized well known comrades from the fort. We recognized Major Smith as in command of the rescue party, and also our genial post surgeon, Dr. Samuel M. Horton, and when they arrived within two hundred yards of us we ran out to meet them, and such a shaking of hands as there was. The first question he asked us was, "Who's hit? Who's killed or wounded?" Our rescuers told us they had not expected to find a man of us alive.

Dr. Horton—God bless him!—for he was also so kind and considerate of every man, woman and child at the post, had his ambulance driven near to the west end of the corral, and with the consent of Captain Powell he gave every man-soldier and civilian—a big drink of whiskey out of a small keg which he had brought along.

Then we tenderly laid the body of Lieutenant Jenness in the ambulance, and the bodies of Doyle and Haggerty in one of the wagons, and having packed our tentage, bedding and rations in the empty wagons, marched back to the fort. When we arrived at the big hill at the west end of the ridge east of the corral, we halted, and as we looked back up Big Piney valley, we saw a long train of Indian ponies, three and four deep and fully a quarter of a mile long. They were carrying off their dead and wounded.

As we approached the commanding officer's quarters, he stepped from the house and halted us. We came to attention and the general removed his cap and complimented Captain Powell and. all of us for our splendid victory against such overwhelming odds. He furthermore added that we had displayed such heroic courage and bravery that he would recommend every one of us for a medal of honor. The recommendation was made, but for some reason none of us ever received the medal.

As to the number of Indians killed in the fight, that is a hard question to answer. Captain Powell, in his official report, estimated the Indian loss at over three hundred killed and wounded, but we—the men of Company C—estimated that there must have been seven or eight hundred killed and wounded. The late General Grenville M. Dodge said that about thirty years ago, in an interview with Chief Red Cloud at Pine Ridge Reservation, the chief placed the total loss of the Sioux, Cheyennes and Arapahoes at over eleven hundred in killed and wounded. It was utterly impossible to keep any account of the individual Indians each man saw fall, because as fast as an Indian dropped, others would ride up and carry him away. Chief Rain-in-the-Face told me at Standing Rock agency in 1895, through an interpreter, that he did not care to talk about the Wagon Box fight.

I have served in the army forty-eight years, taking active part in the Sioux campaign of 1876 and also in the Wounded Knee campaign of 1890-'91 at Pine Ridge agency, but never before or since have my nerves ever been put to the test they sustained on that terrible 2d of August, I 867, when we fought Red Cloud's warriors in the wagon box corral.

The Wagon Box Fight As I Saw It
by Max Littman
Twenty-seventh U.S. Infantry

I enlisted in the United States Army March 20, 1866, having emigrated from Germany but a short time previously. From New York I was sent to Jefferson Barracks, St. Louis, where all recruits were sent at that time. Here we received our guns. From St. Louis we were sent to Fort Leavenworth, and we marched from that post in full battalion. We rested for a time at Fort Kearney, Nebraska, then moved up the North Platte River to Julesburg, or old Fort Sedgwick, as it was then known. From that point we were sent to Fort Laramie, where we again rested. We then marched almost due north to the site of Fort Reno, and from there to the site of Fort Phil Kearney.

I was twenty-one years of age at that time and unable to speak the English language at all. However, I was desirous of seeing something of the country to the west before making any attempt to establish myself in business. In seven months after I enlisted I was made sergeant of my company, although I had not by any means mastered the language. All my orders for my company were written down for me in English, which I memorized word for word.

Passing over different events which happened at Fort Phil Kearney during my stay there, I will come down to the famous Wagon Box fight of August 2, 1867. My company had been detailed to guard the woodchoppers in the pinery while getting out logs to finish some of the fort buildings, and also to use for fuel. On the morning of August 2, I was stationed at the wagon box corral, which was under the command of Captain James Powell. Part of the men were off guard, myself among the number, and we were lounging in our tents on the south side of the corral.

Suddenly we heard a commotion, followed by a cry of "Indians!" We who were in the tents immediately ran out to see what was the matter. I looked to the south where the pickets were stationed, and saw Captain Powell running up from the creek where he had been taking a bath. Upon seeing the Indians swarming down over the hills, he hurried to give the alarm, as did those who were on picket duty.

We were immediately ordered into the corral. There were twenty-five soldiers, two officers and five civilians, or teamsters, making thirty-two men all told. Captain Powell reported that there were several thousand rounds of ammunition in boxes, besides which, every man had forty rounds in his belt, so that we had plenty of ammunition to use. The gun we were using was a breech-loading Springfield rifle—a style of weapon entirely unknown to the Indians up to that day, and we had only received them two or three weeks previously, but had not had an opportunity to try them against the Indians. It was the rapidity with which we were enabled to deliver our fire that puzzled and drove back the vast hordes of savages which repeatedly charged us. In addition to our rifles, every man also was armed with a revolver, but we did not use them—not, at least to my knowledge.

After being ordered into the corral, most of the men at once got inside the wagon boxes to fight it out with the Indians from behind this slight barricade. It occurred to me, however, that those wagon boxes—which were nothing but very thin planks—were mighty poor protection when it came to stopping a bullet, so I hastily looked around for some better protection. I found a barrel half full of salt. This I wheeled into position, and on the top I piled several neck-yokes used on the oxen, which afforded me some better protection than the wagon boxes alone. Flat on my stomach behind this barrel of salt, I did all my fighting, and another soldier named Jim Condon was lying next to me behind a barrel of beans, where he used his rifle in a most determined and dextrous [*sic*] manner.

An erroneous impression has been made by some historians and other writers who have attempted to give to the public the details of this most extraordinary engagement. They have stated that the wagon boxes used in this fight were lined with boiler iron and had loop holes in the sides. It also has been said that the wagon boxes were made entirely of iron. All of this is absolutely untrue. They were just the ordinary wooden wagon box, without a bit of iron or any other protection about them. They stood about four or five feet high, and the fighting was all done over the tops of the boxes, and not through any loopholes or any other such contrivance. If there was any wagon box in that fight that had been specially fortified or made bullet proof, I did not see it nor hear anything about it. There were no sacks of corn nor grain stuffed between the boxes to stop bullets, either. There were sacks of grain for the oxen and mules inside the corral, but there was no time to pile up such a barricade before the savages descended in hundreds upon us.

The reader must remember that two persons will often see things in an entirely different light; and for that reason I am stating only what came under my own personal observation in this fight. Some of our men were facing to the west, some to the north and others to the south, consequently different things were happening at different points of the compass, and some men saw and noted things which did not come under the observation of their comrades. This was due to the fact that this corral was oblong in shape, and we faced in different directions.

When we saw the hundreds upon hundreds of savage warriors pressing forward against our little improvised fort, not a man in the entire command expected to come out of that fight alive. The battle could not positively have lasted half an hour longer than it did for we were almost completely exhausted by the awful heat of the day, and from the smoke occasioned by the fire arrows which the savages shot into the corral, and which ignited with scattered bits of hay and dry manure which had collected—for it was inside this corral where our animals were kept at night to prevent their being stampeded and run off by the Indians. This terrible stench and smoke nearly strangled us at times.

All the charges that I saw made against us by the Indians were on foot. True, they were on their ponies when they came down the mountain-sides and across the country, but the ponies were left out of rifle range, with their squaws to attend them, and the advances were all made without them—at least all that came under my observation. Many of the Indians circled us on their ponies and shot arrows into the corral in this manner, but they did not make a direct charge on horseback.

The first advance against us was made from the north hills. There were about three hundred Indians in this initial advance. They were stripped naked, save for breech-cloth and moccasins, and were all hideously painted for the fray. Their surplus clothing and fancy decorations were laid aside during the battle. They advanced on foot, very slowly at first, and after the first volley fired by our men on the north side of the corral—ten to fifteen in number—the savages advanced on the run. At the second volley the Indians still came on with wild cries and shrill warwhoops, thinking, no doubt, that once our guns were empty they could break over the corral and score an easy victory. But at the third volley they broke and fled for the hills out of rifle range. They had expected a time to expire after the first volley was delivered, and could not understand the rapid and continuous shooting without, apparently, stopping to reload. They advanced to within two hundred feet of the corral before the third volley sent them scattering. Had they advanced steadily with their entire force—which could not have numbered much under three thousand braves—the fight would not have lasted five minutes. It would have been simply impossible on our part to have loaded and fired rapidly—enough to have prevented hundreds of them passing over our slight barricade, and had they once got inside the corral, it would have been all over in no time. It was perhaps a pardonable timidity on their part, as they had never before encountered breech-loading guns—and I am not speaking of repeating rifles, such as are used in the present day, but of single-loaders.

I kept my gun pretty well heated up during the conflict. I observed one huge Indian who seemed to have singled me out as his special foe. He was armed only with bow and arrows, but he certainly knew how to use his primitive weapons in a most skillful manner. Every time he sent a shaft at me he would leap into the air as high as he could, and would deliver his arrow; at the apex of the leap. He was located not to exceed thirty to fifty feet away from me, but was in a slight depression into which I could not send an effective bullet. The only chance I had to return his fire would be when he jumped into the air to shoot at me. I fired at him a great many times before I finally managed to send a bullet where it would do the most good to all concerned.

I was stationed at the southwest corner of the corral, and in the excitement of the fight some of the Indians managed to get within five or six feet of us before falling under the withering fire we poured into them. These bodies falling so close to the corral, were not removed by their companions. Indians always recover their dead whenever possible, but these warriors were too close to our dead-line for any such attempt at rescue by their companions.

Early in the fight Lieutenant Jenness fell. He was standing behind the wagon boxes at the extreme west end of the corral, and was looking toward the west. He was just remarking, "Boys, look out! There are a good many Indians here, but—" The sentence was never finished. A bullet struck him in the head, killing him instantly. I was just at his left, kneeling to fire from behind my salt barrel when he received the fatal shot.

During the fight many of the men suffered greatly for want of water, of which we had no time to get a supply when attacked. As for myself, I was not thirsty, and did not use a drop of water during the entire battle; neither did the man stationed at my left.

Just after Lieutenant Jenness was killed, a mule was shot directly to my right. I worked my way over to the carcass and tried to pull it over where it would protect the body of my lieutenant from further mutilation, as a great many shots were being fired from the north. The mule, however, was too heavy for me to budge, and I had to give it up.

So far as I know, there were no blankets placed over the tops of the wagon boxes as protection from flying arrows. These shafts, more often than not, had burning pitch tied to them. Many of them dropped inside the corral and started the loose hay into flame and smudge. There was at least a smouldering [sic] fire burning in the center of the corral most of the time, and, as stated else-where, this smudge, smoke and stench would almost strangle us at times. The Indians not only were armed with bows and arrows, but they had guns as well. They had the eighty-one weapons secured from the Fetterman fight of December 21 the previous year. They also had obtained firearms from the wagon trains which they had successfully attacked along the Bozeman Trail, for the white man's tragedy along this road afforded the red men many weapons. Isolated trappers and frontiersmen also had been killed at various times and their guns secured. The Indians had further managed to acquire rifles from white traders while trafficking for buffalo robes and other peltries.

No person inside the corral was killed by an arrow. It was always a bullet that did the deadly work. However, our losses were very slight, and it seems almost beyond belief that it was a case of but thirty-two desperate men against three thousand infuriated Sioux. They must have lacked the right sort of leader, for had they attacked us in full force at any one time, not a man of us would have been spared except to be reserved for torture.

I have seen somewhere a statement that one man used eight guns throughout this fight. This may have been true, but I did not see it myself, if any such incident occurred.

The first news we had that relief was coming from the fort was about one o'clock in the afternoon. We heard a cannon-shot and a shell exploded very close to where the main body of savages were congregated. At this shot the Indians fled from the field, going toward the northwest, from which direction they had first appeared.

The Indians were very brave in this fight, but seemed to lack a good leader, and did not use judgment in their attacks. I did not see any of our men jump to their feet and hurl any augurs or tools or stones into the faces of the Indians, as some writers have pictured.

No such battle as this has ever been recorded in all the Indian engagements of the west—I mean, where the whites were so overwhelmingly outnumbered—and we were outnumbered nearly a hundred to one. Neither has there been such a successful combat with Indians anywhere in the United States as to numbers killed in comparison to those fighting against them. The closest approach to it was the Beecher

Island fight on the Arickaree Fork of the Republican River in 1868, where fifty men stood off about seven hundred Cheyennes for several days before relief came. The more one goes into the details of the fight, the more deeply is one impressed that it was the greatest Indian battle of the world. Thirty-two men struggling for six hours against three thousand well trained, dogged Indians—and the lesser number without any entrenchments, and with but the most meager protection. It cannot be emphasized too strongly that there was no entrenching done from the time of the sounding of the alarm to the time of the bursting of the first shell fired by the relief party from Fort Phil Kearney.

Referring to other matters of interest about old Fort Phil Kearney, I should state that I not only helped construct this post, but was one of the soldiers who stayed through its entire existence. I left the post with my company during August, 1868. From there we marched on foot to Cheyenne, and cheer after cheer went up when we heard the whistle of a locomotive, which the year before had made its appearance in that frontier town. From Cheyenne we took a train to a point in Nebraska. It must be remembered that we walked all the way from Fort Leavenworth to Fort Phil Kearney two years before. My company was mustered out at Plum Creek, Nebraska, and I was then detailed to Elm Creek, twelve miles east.

In speaking of the signals which Colonel Carrington installed for use at Fort Phil Kearney, I would state that the hill known today as Pilot Hill was the spot where these signals were displayed. On this point was a platform, and the back of the platform was in the manner of an entrenchment. The Indians signaled from their vantage points with mirrors. The soldiers signaled to the fort and other points with flags. Two of the signals were as follows: If a train of emigrants was seen on the Bozeman Trail, either going northwest or returning southeast, the flag was started at the ground and raised ninety degrees to zenith, and then wagged back to the ground again and furled back over the heads of the soldiers. If Indians were sighted on the trail or elsewhere, the flags executed a circle of one hundred and eighty degrees, starting from the ground on one side and going to the zenith and over to the ground on the reverse side, then back again and over again.

I knew old Jim Bridger, the famous scout and guide, very well, as he was the government guide for our battalion. He was at that time dressed in buckskin clothing. He was five feet, ten or eleven inches tall, of slim build, and was then sixty-two years of age. When one looked into his eyes they were wonderfully keen, and he could turn them down almost to a bead. He was silent when scouting, and knew every Indian sign and indication of the surrounding foe.

After 1869 my army life on the plains was a thing of the past. I was a young man and had my living to make. From that time until 1908 I had practically forgotten everything in connection with my army and Indian experiences. That year my son—who lives in St. Louis, saw something in the papers about a reunion which General Carrington was attending at Sheridan, Wyoming, in connection with the Fetterman Massacre Memorial monument and the battleground near old Fort Phil Kearney on the Bozeman Trail. Until I saw this notice, I did not know the general was still alive. I wrote to him at Hyde Park, Mass., where I found he was then living. Later, I learned that Sergeant Samuel Gibson, with whom I fought Indians on the plains, was living in Omaha. Gibson was in my company, and was himself in the Wagon Box fight. After that, he paid me a visit at St. Louis, and there we re-fought the Wagon Box battle in memory.

The United States government at one time promised that all the survivors of this wonderful engagement against hostile Indians would be rewarded with appropriate medals. Recognition, however, of the bravery and gallantry of our little handful of soldiers never has been made, and doubtless never will be. In any event, the Wagon Box fight seems to have been totally forgotten, save by the very few now alive who participated in that thrilling engagement.

My Experience In The Wagon Box Fight
by Frederic Claus
Twenty-seventh Infantry

I arrived in New York City from Germany at the age of twenty-six. Times were hard, and so, early in 1867, I enlisted in the army. I was sent immediately to Fort McPherson, and from there, as soon as possible, with reinforcements, to Fort Phil Kearney, going over the road on foot, via Fort Laramie, Fort Fetterman and Fort Reno. The Eighteenth Regiment U.S. Infantry was at that time stationed—one battalion at Fort Reno and the other at Fort Phil Kearney. Part of our reinforcements were put in the Eighteenth, at Fort Reno and the balance at Fort Phil Kearney, where they were made into the Twenty-seventh U.S. Infantry.

When our reinforcements reached Fort Phil Kearney, I and some others were attached to Company C, Twenty-seventh U.S. Infantry, under Captain James W. Powell. Company C was detailed to the woods to protect the woodchoppers and the wagon train, which carried the logs from the pinery to the fort, also accompanying the empty wagons back. The wagon boxes were not used, but were taken off the gears and formed into an oval shaped corral. These wagon boxes were placed a little north of our tents.

On that memorable 2d of August, 1867, after the wagon train with the guards had been gone perhaps a couple of hours, the pickets gave the alarm of "Indians!" Captain Powell was down at the creek, taking a bath, I believe. He came toward the corral on the run, shouting: "Boys, the Indians are here! I It will be a hard day for you all. You know what your orders are !"

Lieutenant Jenness called the company—or what was left of it, to fall in line, and the orderly-sergeant told us to take the ammunition out of the wagons and distribute it around in the wagon boxes, and to seek shelter in them at once. The lieutenant had not been very long in the country, and had had no experience in fighting Indians. He was instructed to also get in one of the wagon boxes where he would be sheltered from the fire of the Indians, but he replied that he knew how to fight redskins as well as anyone. This was his last sentence, for just then he fell dead with a bullet through his brain. That was in the first charge the Indians made, where they posted their sharpshooters in front of the wagon boxes with bows and arrows and tried to set them on fire.

We had to contend with a rifle with which we were not acquainted. They were breech-loaders, and we had received them only about two weeks previously. We knew that our only salvation was in keeping the Indians from getting inside the corral. Once there, and they could easily have cleaned us all up. The air was so full of smoke from our guns that it was seldom that we could see further than a few rods, and we had to be very careful in putting our heads above the wagon boxes in order to shoot.

Sometimes a box was set on fire by the Indians when they would shoot fire arrows into them. Large bodies of the savages were lying close in front of the wagon beds, where they could easily reach our position with their primitive weapons, and large numbers of them were also armed with rifles.

These wagon boxes from which we were fighting were just the old fashioned prairie schooner style. None of them were lined with boiler iron, nor anything else which would serve to protect us. I have read stories by some writers that these wagon boxes were especially prepared for just such a fight as we were engaged in. but they were not. None of them had sides which were more than an inch thick, through which bullets whizzed as easily as if we had no protection at all.

At the beginning of the fight, our tents were pulled down by some of the men to give us better observation to the south, and which left no place behind which the Indians could skulk up closer to us.

The woodchoppers who had been cut off in the woods and were unable at the time to reach our wagon box fort, hid out in the timber until the fight was over, and then they came in and went to the fort with us.

When the reinforcements arrived from the fort, we were indeed a happy lot of men. None of us ever expected to come out of that fight alive. There was a howitzer with the relief party, and it dealt death and destruction to the savages and put them quickly to flight.

I have read somewhere in some magazine about the number of Indians which are said to have been killed in this fight, and the figures given were between twelve hundred and thirteen hundred. This sounds to me pretty unreasonable and overdrawn, and I cannot believe their loss was so great as that. As I remember it, we found only one wounded Indian which they were unable to carry away with them. There was also a dead mule inside our corral. Our own loss was two or three killed and several wounded, but it was very slight in comparison to the Indian loss which must have amounted to several score. It must also be remembered that we had only thirty-two men fighting, and the Indian force was in the neighborhood of three thousand warriors.

Some months after the battle I and another comrade spoke to an Indian who had come to the fort. He could speak a little English. We asked him how many warriors Red Cloud had in the Wagon Box fight, and the Indian gave the number as over two thousand five hundred fighting men. Then we asked him how many Red Cloud lost. He could not—or would not—tell, but stated that the chief had declared that he lost the flower of his nation, and we came to the conclusion that their loss must have been a couple of hundred at least. I said always that it was impossible for our thirty-two men to have killed thirteen hundred out of their two thousand five hundred warriors.

There were many interesting happenings at Fort Phil Kearney, as well as sad ones, but after a lapse of fifty years and more, many of them have escaped my memory and I am unable to recall them. The Wagon Box fight, however, is something that can never be effaced from my memory while time shall last.

A Summary of Historical Archaeology at the Wagon Box Site[*]

Mark E. Miller, Danny N. Walker, and Jeffrey L. Hauff

Preface

Although the archaeological summary that follows is intended to supplement the foregoing account of the Wagon Box Fight, readers should realize that it is a self-contained study, prepared as a separate work. Accordingly, all conclusions and interpretations are solely those of the authors.

With regard to the report itself, readers will note a difference in the archaeological method of citing sources, as opposed to that found in the historical narrative preceding this report. Data in parentheses refers to the source for that statement. Thus, "Wallace" (1968:173) refers to Anthony F. C. Wallace, *The Anthropology of Armed Conflict*, page 173). A number preceded by "Keenan" refers to the page in the foregoing text where that topic is discussed. Thus, (Keenan, 25 refers to page 25 in this volume).

---

[*] A gallery of pages related to archaeological surveys conducted at the site of the Wagon Box Fight is found at the end of this appendix.

Finally, because it is a self-contained study, the archaeological report also includes its own bibliography.

It is hoped that the inclusion of this material will provide readers with an additional dimension from which to better understand the Wagon Box Fight.

Mark E. Miller
Danny N. Walker
Jeffrey L. Hauff

Introduction

Warfare is the most violent means that cultural groups use to resolve conflict, so the study of combat behavior is integral to understanding the full range of the human experience. As anthropologist Anthony F. C. Wallace (1968:173) reminded us during the Vietnam conflict, nearly every society in the history of the world has engaged in at least one war during its existence. United States expansion in the American West during the nineteenth century is no exception. That period chronicles a series of brutal military engagements that produced battlefield landscapes throughout the region. Sites like the Wagon Box Fight are a tangible legacy of unconventional warfare that underscores vast cultural differences between Native Americans and New World immigrants; a legacy not even addressed in some historical studies (Limerick, 1987, 1995:124). Even so, battlefields are a part of our cultural heritage that can be viewed more clearly through interdisciplinary research that includes the archaeological record.

One of the most provocative issues in the history of the Wagon Box Fight on August 2, 1867, is the exact location of the corral during the engagement. In the foregoing account, Jerry Keenan discusses a lingering controversy that developed between eyewitness participants attempting to relocate the defense perimeter years after the battle. One popular site is the state monument in Sheridan County, and another is the pipe marker in Johnson County. Historical documents are ambiguous on this issue, so the archaeological record was investigated to help resolve the dispute.

Distinctive artifact distributions are expected at Indian wars battlefields because the combatants were culturally different. On one side was the U. S. Army, which had just fought the Civil War using antiquated tactics by massing thousands of soldiers into exposed positions and then firing into the ranks at close range with state-of-the-art weapons. This was a perilous combination that stretched casualty figures to astronomical heights. In spite of these losses, scores of battle-scarred veterans brought their Civil War experiences out west, initially believing the tactics that beat the Rebels could easily conquer the Indians.

On the other side were independent societies of Native Americans who had lived in various parts of North America for thousands of years, although many prominent tribes were only recent arrivals to the High Plains. Their warfare often employed a guerrilla strategy with hit-and-run tactics, frequently attempting to lure large numbers of the enemy into planned ambuscades. The introduction of firearms and horses to these groups increased the lethality of conflicts and geographic expansion that precipitated encounters long before the arrival of the U. S. Army (see Mishkin, 1940; Reher and Frison, 1980; Secoy, 1992). Generations of intertribal warfare honed their military skills and made them wary of any territorial intrusion. To at least one Indian wars scholar, these two sides were so wholly dissimilar that there was hardly any opportunity for mediation (Marshall, 1972:2). The Wagon Box Fight is only one result of failed compromise during this period of history.

Archaeology and Battlefield Pattern Recognition

The theoretical model of battlefield archaeology assumes diagnostic artifacts and their spatial distribution will yield specific clues about combatants and tactical behavior. This assumption enables archaeologists to detect battlefield positions occupied by each opposing force during an engagement (Fox and Scott, 1991). Culturally different forces should exhibit different types of weapons, ammunition, personal items, and livestock equipment. Specific artifact types like these are assumed to have been used for particular purposes and their undisturbed archaeological context allows the development of inferences regarding their function in combat episodes.

The model also assumes: (1) arrows tipped with metal points were fired as projectiles at enemy targets; (2) cartridge cases are the by-product of firing particular caliber bullets; and (3) where an artifact was found is the location where a specific activity took place. Since an arrowhead or bullet lands at the end of its firing trajectory, several projectiles in the same general area may reflect a target position, although over shots must be taken into account (Smith, 1995:122). A cartridge case drops where it was ejected following a gun discharge, and several cartridge cases in linear array may reflect a skirmish line or other organized firing. Changes in these patterns suggest individual and group maneuvers during a battle. Regularized changes or sustained patterns suggest systematic, tactical stability, while erratic dispersals suggest tactical disintegration and chaos. All of these assumptions acknowledge that post-depositional processes (what happens to items and landscapes over time) can disperse artifacts from their original location and obscure any cultural pattern.

Early perspectives were rather pessimistic regarding the research potential of battlefield archaeology. Hume (1968:188) argued "Little can usefully be said about battlefield sites . . . the salvage of relics becomes the be all and end all." However, a more optimistic assessment emerged a decade later when South (1977) stimulated innovative thinking that led investigators to place greater emphasis on the context and provenience of combat items.

South (1977:158-160) discussed the notion of a battlefield pattern in historical archaeology during his assessment of Ferguson's (1975) work at Fort Watson, South Carolina. A battle had been fought there between American and British soldiers in 1781 that produced a high incidence of arms-related artifacts, such as musket balls, gun flints, and gun parts. The high percentage of distorted rifle balls (62.2 %) suggested a battlefield context where projectiles flattened on impact after firing during an extensive fusillade. The fewer, undistorted balls (37.8%) could have been dropped during weapon loading or lost from supplies. Investigators also used the weight and rifling of lead balls to classify American versus British ammunition. Lead balls shot by the Americans were found to concentrate along two sides of the fort interior, which helped investigators locate a previously unidentified sharpshooter position (South, 1977:79). South (1977:160) suggested that the Fort Watson data represented a "Revolutionary War Military Battle Pattern."

This type of research was greatly expanded in Fox and Scott's (1991) model of a "Post-Civil War Battlefield Pattern" developed for Custer's final fight in 1876 on the Little Bighorn River in southern Montana. They identified two levels of pattern recognition, gross and dynamic. Both require the assumption that site formation processes have not significantly altered artifact distributions.

Gross patterning derives from a relatively coarse grained analysis that identifies combat positions and battle episodes at fixed locations on the landscape. It is predominantly synchronic and seeks correlation of evidence for events by comparing the archaeological record to the historical record. Dynamic patterning is finer grained and tracks specific individual, unit, or firearm movements through time across the landscape by using firearms identification analysis. It attempts to identify distinctive ammunition attributes such as firing-pin, extractor, and land-and-groove marks to trace movements or trajectories of specific firearms over the battlefield. This type of analysis requires the expertise of firearms and ballistics specialists commonly employed by state or private crime laboratories.

Haecker and Mauck (1997) recently applied the theoretical framework of battlefield pattern to the 1846 engagement at Palo Alto fought during the Mexican War. In doing so, they emphasize obvious differences between pre-Civil War and post-Civil War armaments, such as smoothbore versus rifled barrels, paper cartridges with round lead balls versus metallic cartridge cases with conical lead bullets, and the relative importance of small arms versus artillery at individual engagements. These differences prompted their recognition of the battlefield pattern at Palo Alto as one more typical of the "smooth bore period," and more reflective of eighteenth-century European warfare than the American Civil War (Haecker and Mauck, 1997:9). Their terminology for pattern recognition emphasizes weapons technology rather than warfare chronology, and underscores the influence that different armaments have on artifact distributions.

Battlefield pattern recognition must take into account several attributes of the archaeological record and the human behavior that produced the record. Weapons technology is only one area of research that helps define a battlefield pattern; different strategic, tactical, and cultural behaviors influence patterns as well. For example, was one side totally annihilated; was there a sustained defensive position or mobile skirmishing; was there time to execute tactical maneuvers; were mounted soldiers involved or only foot soldiers; which Native American tribes participated; were civilians involved; were combatants good marksmen or were many targets missed? These are only a few factors that may influence the spatial structure of a battlefield pattern.

History of Archaeological Investigations at the Wagon Box Fight

Evidence at the Wagon Box Fight (site number 48SH129) is just beginning to add to the growing number of studies on battlefield archaeology, although scholars have known about the research potential at the site for most of this century (Miller et. al., 1997; Reiss and Scott, 1984). Charles E. Bezold found cartridge cases there in 1908 after discussing the location with Sam Gibson, a veteran of the engagement (Keenan, 25). Dr. Grace Raymond Hebard eventually had Bezold's artifacts analyzed and identified as the type used by soldiers in the battle. Hebard and Bezold visited the site again in 1916 and found even more items (Keenan, 26, 32) also illustrates artifacts found even later by Sterling Fenn, another prominent historian. We are continuing to contact informants about artifact collections from the battlefield and the database of known artifact locations is growing.

A few early investigators mapped the distribution of their artifact discoveries, which strengthens the analytical potential of their finds. J. W. Vaughn collected eleven cartridge cases of the Springfield .50-70 type, some .44 caliber cases, a wagon ring, and a carbine sling buckle (Vaughn, 1967; Reiss and Scott, 1984:68). Don Rickey collected artifacts between 1956-1958 and reported six to eight .50-70 cases of the type used by soldiers in the battle, and four to five .50 caliber Spencer rimfire cases (Reiss and Scott, 1984:68-69). These Vaughn and Rickey cartridge cases are incorporated into the artifact distribution maps that are presented later in this report. Also included in these maps are a cartridge case and bullets found by Reiss and Scott (1983:24, 1984:70), who completed the first attempt by professional archaeologists to systematically survey the one acre of state property with metal detectors and record the point provenience of each item. Their discoveries include 46 artifacts that may be related to the battle, including square nails, rivets, horse shoe nails, round lead musket balls, a .50-70 cartridge case of the type used by soldiers in the battle, a metal buckle, and a metal ring (Reiss and Scott, 1984:70). A later metal detection survey of the access road into the state monument area produced no additional battle-related artifacts (Eckles, 1984).

Cartridge cases gathered by the mid-1980s led researchers to an important observation relative to the two different marker locations established to commemorate the Wagon Box Fight—ammunition found near the state monument in Sheridan County was of the type used by the soldiers in the battle, while cases found at the pipe marker in Johnson County were not even manufactured until after the fight (Keenan, 33; Reiss and Scott, 1984:67).

Overview of the 1993-1994 Project

Differences between artifacts from the two marked locations, and the desire to provide better public interpretation at the Wagon Box Fight, prompted a cooperative research effort between the Fort Phil Kearny–Bozeman Trail Association (FPK/BTA), the Office of the Wyoming State Archaeologist (OWSA), and the State Parks and Historic Sites Division (SPHS) of the Wyoming Department of Commerce. Staff archaeologists and volunteers conducted two 10-day field sessions in 1993-1994 to document archaeological evidence for the 1867 battle. The crew surveyed approximately 40 acres of the battlefield with metal detectors, including areas adjacent to the state monument in Sheridan County and the pipe marker in Johnson County (Figure 1, p. 118). These markers were considered important research locations because of the controversy regarding the actual location of the Wagon Box corral (Hilman, 1941; Keenan; Miller et. al., 1997). A primary goal of this research was to use gross pattern analysis to identify where the Wagon Box corral might have been located during the battle.

Field methods were adopted from those used in the project at the battle of the Little Bighorn (Scott and Fox, 1987, Scott, et. al., 1989), and are described elsewhere (Miller et. al., 1997:13-15). Survey parameters evolved considerably between 1993 and 1994 because of changing elements in the research design. Initially, a block of approximately 22 acres of land north of the Sheridan/Johnson county line and south of an irrigation ditch below a prominent ridge slope was intended for survey. Most of this area was surveyed in 1993 and it surrounds the one acre of fenced state land surveyed by Reiss and Scott (1984). Field work in 1994 covered the western margin of the FPK/BTA property and additional acreage on private land in Johnson County. Twenty-two 50 meter x 50 meter grids were surveyed around the pipe marker and along the irrigation ditch in Johnson County. Three 50 meter x 50 meter blocks were added adjacent to the southwest corner of the 1993 survey to completely cover the Wishart fortification. An additional trapezoidal parcel (approximately two 50 meter x 50 meter blocks) was surveyed near a rock outcropping west of the irrigation ditch in Johnson County. The combined survey area for the two year period was nearly 40 acres.

Artifact Analysis

One thousand seven hundred and forty-three (1,743) survey points were recorded with an Electronic Distance Measurement (EDM) instrument during the project. Many of these shots were key topographic points needed to document the contours of the battlefield (Figure 1). However, 1,092 shots represent artifacts discovered during metal detection transects. Modern items discovered, such as fence staples, flip-tops from aluminum cans, bottle caps, and other recent trash, were removed from the site. The remaining artifacts, most believed to be contemporary with the Wagon Box Fight, were analyzed and cataloged. Selected artifacts are discussed here, while the rest of the assemblage is described in detail elsewhere (Miller et. al., 1997).

Battlefield Ammunition

Cartridge components of the .50-70-450 variety commonly occur in the archaeological record of late nineteenth century sites throughout Wyoming. Two attributes are sufficiently unique to identify this specific cartridge and three are identifiable only to caliber. The first two attributes are primer morphology and the crimp pattern on the cartridge case. The last three are the size of the case and the diameter and weight of the conical lead bullet. All five have been detected in the military ammunition discarded at the Wagon Box Fight. These cartridges are the principal diagnostic items for identifying possible U. S. Army firing positions and bullet trajectories during the battle.

The shoulderless (straight body) cartridge case is copper, slightly conical at the mouth due to swaging around the bullet, and bears no headstamp. Firing can straighten out the conical taper, so this attribute may be imperceptible on spent cases found in the archaeological record. The case has an internal primer—an iron bar—held in place by two crimping grooves 0.110 inches from the base of the case rim; the indents are 0.480 inches apart (Lewis, 1972:29-31).

Twenty-three cartridge cases of the .50-70 Government type with bar anvil primers were found on the Wagon Box battlefield during 1993-1994 (Miller et. al., 1997:22) (Figure 2, p. 119). Firing pin marks are particularly deep on these cartridge case heads, with noticeably sharp margins where the pin tip terminated at maximum penetration. Sharply defined firing pin marks are not unexpected considering the rifles were newly issued to the soldiers and had not begun to show wear from repeated use. According to at least one authority (James Harrell, personal communication, 1995), the early Springfield firing pin design may have tended to perforate the cartridge heads causing severe problems when the powder ignited. Firing pins eventually may blunt through heavy use thus limiting the depth of perforation, so marks from a worn firing pin should be more shallow and exhibit rounded terminations.

Since attributes of firing pin marks may help link cartridge cases to the new weapons used in the Wagon Box Fight, an attempt was made to compare depths on these specimens to those from cases at a different military site, Fort Fred Steele (Miller and Wedel, 1992). Fort Fred Steele was occupied between 1868-1886, but the garrison may not have received .45 caliber Springfields until well after 1873, so many of the earlier .50 caliber weapons probably were in use for some time. A firing range at Fort Fred Steele produced 63 cartridge cases of the .50 caliber bar anvil type. These were compared with 21 measurable specimens from the Wagon Box Fight (Figure 3, p. 120). Firing pin depths were taken by maximum insertion of a narrow diameter, metal rod secured in the frame of a contour gauge. The length of the rod was then measured by dial calipers to the nearest 0.001 inch. As expected, the Wagon Box cartridge cases clearly had deeper firing pin penetrations, and appeared to exhibit sharper terminations although this attribute was not measured.

The Martin tinned iron bar anvil primer is shaped somewhat like a miniature, double-bladed axe head. It has a fulminate cavity in the center and convex ends that are grooved to receive the crimped indents on the cartridge case when the primer is set in place. Published dimensions for these primers have not been found, but four bar anvil primers recovered at the Wagon Box Fight average 0.530 mm in maximum length, 0.226 mm in maximum width, and 0.159 mm in maximum thickness (Miller et. al., 1997:24). Only the Wagon Box defenders would have had access to these items on the battlefield in early August 1867.

Eleven other cases are believed to be copper, rimfire Spencer cases from .56/.50, .56/.52, or .56/.56 cartridges (Miller et. al., 1997:25). At least five of these are probably the .56/.50 variety. The .56/.56 Spencer was patented March 6, 1860 and manufactured in quantity as early as 1862, while the .56/.50 cartridge was designed by the Springfield Armory in 1864. The Spencer rifle was a seven shot, lever action repeater (Barnes, 1980:297; Marcot, 1983).

Two Spencer cases from Wagon Box have markings on their case heads. One is believed to be a .56/.52 case with a headstamp labeled VV & Co., which probably is a remnant of FVV & Co. that stands for Fitch, Van

Vechten & Co. (see Barber, 1987:28). Suydam (1960:127, 173) indicates this headstamp is generally found on .56/.52 cases in use during the Civil War, although it occurs on .56/.50 cartridges as well (Sterling Fenn, personal communication, 1996). The other case shows segments of seven lines on either side of the firing pin mark (e.g., Marcot, 1983:222). One of the .56/.50 Spencer's is a complete, unfired cartridge. Native Americans could have had several Spencer carbines taken from the Fetterman battlefield (see Brown, 1971:174) and used them in the Wagon Box Fight, but Spencer's were also used by civilians at the defense perimeter.

Three cases are from .44 caliber Henry cartridges. One of these shows the distinctive double firing pin impression attributable to a Henry rifle or the Model 1866 Winchester (Scott, et. al., 1989:162), and the second is a complete Henry Flat cartridge. Henry Flat cartridges were manufactured as early as 1860-1861 (Barber, 1987:9; Barnes, 1980:296; Logan, 1959:68). This ammunition might have been used by either Native Americans or civilians during the Wagon Box Fight.

The remaining cartridge cases found in 1993-1994 either post-date the Wagon Box Fight or are fragmentary specimens that may or may not be contemporary. They are described elsewhere (Miller et. al., 1997:25).

Bullets

The .50 caliber, 450 grain, conical lead bullet used in U. S. Government cartridges has three grease grooves and a flat to slightly concave base with a shallow central indentation. Manufacturing tolerance allows a weight variance of five grains when bullets leave the arsenal (Lewis, 1972:11), so undeformed specimens may weigh between 445-455 grains. Most of the lead projectiles on the battlefield are heavily deformed with impact modifications and several have fragmented, but seven conical shaped bullets appear to have three grease grooves and diameters suggestive of .50 caliber size (Miller et. al., 1997:24).

Several other bullet calibers may indicate ammunition used by either side in the fight. The largest lead ball in the collection appears to be about a .72 caliber round that shows no pronounced impact deformation, but retains some pitting. It probably is a musket ball fired by a warrior from an early trade rifle.

Eight bullets are the .58 caliber conical minie ball variety probably fired from captured infantry rifles of the Fetterman command (see Brown 1971:175) (e.g., Figure 4, p. 121). Seven of these show the typical three grease groove pattern and basal concavity. Those whose tips have not been deformed by impact also show a distinctive, impressed ring around the nose that was formed by the ramrod head during loading. Loading rings such as these are common on minie balls that were forced into dirty or heavily used breeches, as might occur when a weapon is fired many times in succession without cleaning (Sterling Fenn, personal communication 1996). The eighth bullet believed to be of this caliber shows two grease grooves. This bullet has been cut across the base, removing part of the original bullet, and the basal cavity has been carved out (Figure 4). Perhaps a Native American combatant modified this bullet for reuse, or it may be a Williams Wiper, Type II Minie (U.S. cleaner-type Minie) missing its hard metal base. One of these was included in each pack of ten .58 caliber paper cartridges (Sterling Fenn, personal communication, 1996).

One round bullet with a diameter of 0.564 in. and a conical bullet with three grease grooves are believed to be .56 caliber projectiles. Five lead balls may be .54 caliber, but only two show any impact deformation. One conical bullet with three grease grooves also may be a .54 caliber round. These calibers probably were available to either the Native American warriors or civilians.

Fifty caliber rounds are much more numerous. Besides those mentioned above from the .50-70-450 cartridges, nine conical bullets with two grease grooves and one ball believed to be .50 caliber were identified.

Seven lead balls have been classified as .44 caliber revolver rounds and they typically show sprue projections (excess lead) from their molding stage, ring impressions from contact with ramrods, and striae (minute grooves) from having been fired. Both the attackers and defenders would have had access to 1860 Army Colts using this ammunition (e.g., Haven and Belden, 1940:101; Suydam, 1979). Sterling Fenn (personal communication, 1996) contends that warriors and civilians, rather than the soldiers, are the most likely candidates to have used such crude cast round balls in the Wagon Box Fight. One bullet that may have been conical also measures to approximately a .44 caliber round.

Two lead balls appear to be .36 or .38 caliber revolver rounds. Like the .44 caliber examples, one shows an impression ring from the revolver ramrod and the second a sprue from lead molding. Neither exhibits any obvious impact deformation so they may be unfired rounds. Perhaps the Native Americans or the infantry also had access to the .36 caliber Model 1851 Navy Colt or a similar weapon (e.g., Haven and Belden, 1940:75; Suydam, 1979:13).

Four conical shaped bullets also may be .36 or .38 caliber. One of these has three grooves, two appear to have just one groove, and one has no grooves. This latter example exhibits rifling land-and- groove marks, and may be a relatively recent projectile.

One possibly recent round is a .36 caliber conical bullet with land-and-groove marks from rifling. Another specimen also may be a .36 caliber round, but exhibits heavy tip deformation. Two conical bullets may be .32 caliber rounds and neither shows heavy impact distortion. One heavily deformed bullet is believed to be a recent .22 caliber round. Two bullets are so badly deformed that caliber could not be estimated.

Thirteen items have been classified simply as lead shrapnel. These fragments may or may not be related to the Wagon Box fight and none were sufficiently diagnostic to identify caliber or projectile type.

Iron Arrowheads

Perhaps no other trade object exhibited such a variety of manufacturing sources or enjoyed a greater range of use than did metal arrowheads (Hanson, 1972:2-4). They may be mass produced trade items or fashioned by Native Americans (McGonagle, 1973). Many were probably manufactured at trading posts (Hanson, 1972:4).

Two whole and two fragmentary metal points were recovered from the Wagon Box battlefield during the archaeological study (Figure 5, p. 121). Three of these are complete enough to exhibit haft elements characteristic of common metal point types. Two specimens have serrated haft element (tang) margins similar to one illustrated by Hanson (1972: Figure 1), and the third has a distinctive projection along each basal edge similar to another illustrated by Hanson (1972: Figure 2). Presumably these types were mass produced and traded to Native American populations. The fourth Wagon Box example is a distal blade fragment. All four of the metal projectiles are almost certainly the product of Native American weaponry used during the battle.

Wagon Parts

Historical references mention that fourteen wagon boxes were used to form the corral and an additional wagon with running gear was parked just outside the corral to the west (Keenan,). The most reliable accounts argue that these wagons were predominantly of the military quartermaster variety used during the Civil War (Steffan, 1978:91-93), since J. R. Porter's wood supply contract stipulated that the quartermaster would provide wagons for the operation (Keenan, 5; Sinclair, 1956:5). It is unknown exactly how many army wagons were provided or if the number was sufficient. Civilian wagons, such as the prairie schooner type (Horn, 1974:100-101), also might have been in the vicinity as well (Claus, 1990:84).

Twenty-five metal objects may be wagon parts from vehicles involved in the battle (Miller et. al., 1997: Figures 4.11-4.18). Five are bow staples used to attach the wooden bows to the sideboards of the wagon box. One of these is a lower staple and the rest are upper staples. Three washers are believed to be from axle and hub areas on wagon running gear. Two nuts are from wagon body hardware, presumably from an 1864-style front end (Thomas Lindmier, personal communication, 1996). Three rivets, which are believed to come from various locations on nineteenth century wagons, were collected. Two are body rivets and one is a bolster rivet. Two box rod handle nuts also were recovered, as were two D-rings. One of the D-rings may be from a hame strap or saddle part. The other may be from a trace strap, but seems too light duty for use on a six-mule rigging. Two linchpins were found, one of which is believed to be from a civilian wagon. One each of several other items was recovered; including a hand forged staple, a hand forged drive hook, a 5th–wheel bolster, a singletree hook, a reinforcement strap for a side rail, and a possible spindle part (metal band). Even if all of these items are not related to the Wagon Box Fight, many probably were associated with the intensive transport of logs to the fort between 1866-1868.

Yoke Ring and Chains

Several items that probably relate to the use of draft animals also were found. One large, circular object is identified as an ox-yoke ring (Spivey 1979:26), perhaps from a neck yoke assembly contemporary with the military use of the Fort Phil Kearny area (Miller et. al., 1997: Figure 4.34). Sixteen isolated chain links or chain segments were collected. Twelve of these were single links or half links. Five were chain segments ranging from two links to 16 links per segment that appear to be heavy enough for use in a harness assembly with draft animals, although other functions are possible.

Livestock Shoes

Shoes from horses, mules, and oxen were recovered (Miller et. al.: Figures 4.19-4.21). Mules and oxen were used as draft animals during the construction and maintenance of Fort Phil Kearny (e.g., Keenan), so it is reasonable to assume both were involved in the events of August 2, 1867.

Horses are another matter, however. Since Powell's company was infantry, any evidence for horses during the battle probably reflects Native American involvement. Captured cavalry mounts from Fetterman's command probably were shod, as would be most horses that fell into Sioux or Cheyenne hands from other Euro-American herds. Horses kept by the Indians for any length of time eventually would lose their shoes. In addition, there are many varieties of shoes (Berge, 1980; The Cavalry School, 1988), most of which might be stored and used for decades by ranchers. Consequently, it is difficult to firmly associate this artifact type with the battle.

Thirty livestock shoes were analyzed from the two seasons of research at the scene of the Wagon Box Fight. Twenty-one are horseshoes probably relating to ranching activities in the area that post-date the engagement. Four are mule shoes, two of which exhibit only light wear and therefore are unlikely to be reshoeing discards. Rather they might have been lost or thrown from animal hoofs. The remaining five shoes are for oxen, and two of these also show only light wear. One with light wear has been cut off at the fourth nail hole, removing part of each web, which may have been a therapeutic modification for a hoof ailment. Both this shoe and one other still retain at least one nail similar in morphology to dozens of loose nails found during the project.

Nails

Nails frequently occur in the archaeological record of historic sites. Loose livestock nails were collected at the Wagon Box Fight, as were hand forged and cut nails (Miller et. al., 1997: Figure 4.22). Two hundred twenty-one were classed as nails intended for livestock shoeing and most of these may be the product of modern ranching activities. In fact, there is a stock or hay corral just south of the state monument on the road into the state property where scores of modern horse shoe nails were found.

Eleven square nails may be hand forged, while the rest (359) were grouped as cut nails (Miller et. al., 1997:31-32). Hand forged and cut square nails could be associated with military activities between 1866-1868, although Davis (1990) warns that square nails also have many contemporary uses. Complete specimens range from two penny weight to 140, with the vast majority 10 penny or less. Broken and clenched nails may remain from deteriorated, wooden objects, and well over half of the cut nails are fragmentary. Complete nails often show only minimal modification from hammering or wood penetration, and actually may be unused nails kept for equipment maintenance before they were lost.

Canteens

Two canteen parts were found on the battlefield (Miller et. al., 1997: Figure 4.27). One is the half side of an 1861-style canteen (variant of the 1858 pattern) with a series of concentric rings or corrugations pressed into the metal to make it more resistant to denting (McChristian, 1995:36). It also exhibits a solder seam and beads that once held three equidistant tinned iron sling loops; the loops themselves are missing. The diameter of the canteen half measures greater than 7 inches, consistent with the expected size (McChristian, 1995:90), but it also is bent. The second artifact is a bent, tinned metal canteen spout (McChristian, 1995:36, 90) from an unknown canteen style, although it may be associated with the canteen style just described. The spout measures 1.03 in. long.

Utensils

The infantry tent camp was located to the south, just outside the Wagon Box corral on the morning of the battle (Hebard and Brininstool, 1990:59-60; Keenan, 7). Eyewitnesses recalled that coffee water was being heated up in camp and breakfast had just been completed when the battle began. These activities would have required several kitchen and eating utensils that may have been lost or damaged during the ensuing fight. The area around the defense perimeter, therefore, should contain personal and mess items that were used in camp.

Three cup handles were found in 1993-1994 (Miller et al 1997: Figure 4.28). Two nearly complete specimens measure 90-105 mm (3.5-4.1 in.) in total length, are tapered from a wide top to a narrow bottom, and have rolled wire reinforced edges that would have attached at the top to cups. The bottoms would have been secured by a single rivet, but they are broken just above the rivet placement. These handle types are consistent with Civil War era utensils (McChristian, 1995:100-101).

Two utensil fragments are believed to be the bowl end of spoons. One measures 1.30 in. wide and 2.21 in. long and is broken at the solder point where the handle neck would attach. The bowl is pointed at the tip and similar in outline to the 1874 pattern (McChristian, 1995:215). The second item also may be a spoon end, considering the variety of styles available (McChristian, 1995). It also is pointed, broken at the end adjacent to the area of handle attachment, and measures 1.87 in. wide and 3.04 in. long.

One artifact is spatulate shaped with a narrow neck and may be the proximal handle fragment of a silver table spoon or fork. Another appears to be a fragment of a corroded, spatulate shaped utensil handle, possibly for a spoon. This latter handle resembles a pre-1874 military style (McChristian, 1995:214-215), while the former handle may be a civilian style.

One metal, dinner plate was found that is similar to the military mess plate in use until 1875 (McChristian, 1995:101). It is a tinned iron plate that has been flattened, but was deep dish shaped at one time. It measures about 8.25 in. in diameter. A tinned metal bowl, measuring 6 in. in diameter also was recovered and it too has been flattened (Miller et. al., 1997: Figure 4.29).

Tent Peg

One tent peg recovered resembles those used by the military during the 1860s (Sterling Fenn, personal communication, 1994). Its general morphology is similar to an iron, hand-forged pin found earlier at the Wagon Box Fight (Keenan, 32). The peg found during the 1993-1994 survey measures 179 mm long and 12.9 mm wide (7.0 in. by 0.5 in.) and probably is part of the camp gear related to the general period of the Wagon Box engagement (Miller et. al., 1997: Figure 4.30).

Artifact Distributions at the Wagon Box Battlefield

Distributions of point-plotted artifacts were used to infer possible battle-related events for the Wagon Box Fight (Miller et. al., 1997). Combat on August 2, 1867, would have produced a spatial array of items from several different artifact classes. Assuming the spatial integrity of artifact distributions has not been significantly compromised by subsequent events, the aggregation and dispersal of artifacts used by Native American and U. S. Army participants should help resolve the question of where the Wagon Box defense perimeter was located on the battlefield landscape.

Artifact distributions from each of several classes were used to compare the archaeological record of the pipe marker locality in Johnson County (south of the access road) to the state monument in Sheridan County (north of the road) (Figure 1). These comparisons were expected to lead to a determination of the most likely location of the Wagon Box corral at the time of the engagement. The Wishart fortification on the county line also can be identified by artifact distributions, but its location is most visible because a trench was constructed around the perimeter at the time of occupation (MacAdam, 1996:86; Spear, 1993:38).

The cartridge case array (Figure 6, p. 122) illustrates the distribution of .50-70 cases, bar-anvil primers, Spencer rounds, and other caliber cartridge cases. The spatial arrangement allows specific inferences about firing positions on the battlefield landscape.

There are far more firing positions in the north half of the survey block than in the south half. In fact, neither U. S. Army nor Native American firing positions are indicated for the pipe marker locality in Johnson County. Most of the Spencer and "other" cartridges appear to have been ejected from weapons fired in the vicinity of the Wishart fortification, from between the Wishart fortification and state monument, or between the pipe marker and state monument. Cases in the cluster around the Wishart fortification could easily post-date the Wagon Box Fight by a few days since this new location was never under intense attack. Others may be related to warriors firing into the defense perimeter or civilian defenders firing from the Wagon Box perimeter. The fact that Spencer cases are so widely scattered over the northern two-thirds of the survey block suggests multiple, dispersed firing positions, a pattern more suited to Native American maneuvers during the battle than civilians confined behind the Wagon Box corral. This also is consistent with the likelihood that warriors might have had more Spencer carbines in the battle than did the Wagon Box defenders.

The .50-70 cartridge cases have a similar distribution to other calibers, but the four iron bar anvil primers, diagnostic of the cartridge type used by the soldiers in the battle, were found in a single cluster near the northeastern corner of the state monument fence. These may have dislodged during the firing of .50-70 cartridges or been left behind when copper cases disintegrated. If they were dislodged during firing they probably lie very near firing positions, a factor that supports the state monument area as the defense perimeter. No cartridge cases or bar anvils of the type used by soldiers in the battle were found near the pipe marker in Johnson County.

The high frequency of cartridge cases at the Wishart fortification may be due to activities that took place in the weeks following the battle. Or, some wagon boxes may have been moved to this location after the battle and they may have contained battle related artifacts that later became dispersed at the Wishart fortification. Wishart himself, however, visited the battlefield a couple of days after the engagement and observed that ". . . there was little left of the old wagon-bed defenses. They had been hacked to bits and burned by Red Cloud's warriors following the withdrawal of the troops. All about lay signs of the struggle . . ." (MacAdam, 1996:76). This observation implies that the wagon boxes were so completely destroyed they were not moved, a possibility that should be addressed in future research.

Target positions also are inferred from artifact distributions on the battlefield. Three metal arrowheads were found west of the fenced state monument and one was found inside the Wishart fortification (Figure 7, p. 123). Arrows fired from bows held by archers on foot or horseback will carry much shorter distances if they overshoot targets than would lead bullets fired from rifles. Even so, individual archers could release over a dozen arrows per minute at targets beyond a hundred yards (Hamilton, 1982:113, 138). The close proximity of metal arrowheads to the state monument suggests that this is a more likely target position than the pipe marker. The single arrow at the Wishart fortification may have dislodged from one of the wooden wagon parts if the vehicles used in the battle were moved to this location, or it may have been fired at the new fortification after the Wagon Box battle.

Bullet distributions also probably reflect target positions or overshot trajectories (Figure 7). Minie balls of .58 caliber, presumably fired by warriors using rifles taken after the Fetterman battle, were found widely distributed on the battlefield, including the Wishart fortification, the state monument, and the area north of the pipe marker. Bullets were much more dispersed than either metal arrowheads or cartridge cases, suggesting many weapons and numerous firing trajectories.

Most of the .58 caliber rounds were found west of the state monument. The few at the Wishart fortification may be related to later skirmishing, or like those at the pipe marker locality, they may represent over shots. If those near the pipe marker are over shots, marksmen might have been firing from below the ridge (defined by the irrigation ditch in Figure 7) while aiming at the state monument area. This ridge slope is one of the most likely firing positions indicated by historical accounts (see Hebard and Brininstool, 1990:58). Over shots easily could carry to the pipe marker area if shooters behind the ridge crest fired from ground level toward soldiers looking out over the top of wagon boxes. Trajectories that missed targets would carry bullets well beyond the defense perimeter.

In order to reconstruct possible firing trajectories, the long axis orientation of projectiles found in place was measured relative to magnetic north. Orientation was taken from the proximal to the distal end to estimate the flight path as missiles entered the ground. Unfortunately, this measurement was not always possible due to inadvertent disturbance during artifact recovery. Furthermore, attacks were made on the Wagon Box corral from several directions at different times during the engagement, producing hundreds of firing positions and a complex array of trajectories over individual target positions. Some missiles undoubtedly landed short of targets, while others overshot. The length of each trajectory was not calculated, only the flight path. The correlation between projectile orientation and any target position, therefore, is largely conjectural.

Despite these limitations, the long axis orientation was recorded on four .58 caliber rounds including one near the Wishart fortification (a trajectory of 210 degrees), one north of the pipe marker (190 degrees), and two around the state monument (275 degrees and 315 degrees) (Figure 8, p. 124). The first of these may have been fired from the northeast at occupants of the Wishart fortification after the Wagon Box Fight, or it may have overshot an intended target near the state monument. While the second bullet has a flight trajectory toward the pipe marker from the north, it is possible that this projectile was fired at travelers on the pinery road, believed to have been identified by the distribution of wagon parts discussed elsewhere. The final two .58 caliber bullets probably were fired at targets near the present day state monument. The one along a 275 degree trajectory probably was fired from an eastern rifle position below the ridge (irrigation ditch), and overshot its target to carry beyond the defense perimeter before it struck the ground. This scenario is consistent with historical testimony about Native American firing positions, although other explanations probably can be derived. The bullet along a 315 degree trajectory may have been fired toward the state monument area but landed short, toward the pipe marker area but overshot, or toward the pinery road.

The .50 caliber bullets also are widely dispersed across the landscape and many are presumed to have been fired from soldier weapons during the fight. Their array between the Wishart fortification and state monument, and around the pipe marker area, suggest a series of targets on the battlefield that is consistent with historical accounts relating several Indian attacks from different directions. Four of these bullets produced measurable trajectories (Figure 8), including two near the Wishart fortification (246 degrees and 107 degrees) and two near the pipe marker (358 degrees and 225 degrees). The first one at the Wishart fortification may have been fired from the state monument area northeast of the artifact discovery, but the second apparently was fired from the northwest. The two east of the pipe marker were fired from the north or east, which doesn't suggest any affiliation with either of the traditional Wagon Box corral locations.

Orientation also was taken on the four iron arrowheads (Figure 8), and the three closest to the state monument have trajectories of 210 degrees, 287 degrees, and 250 degrees. If targets were near the state monument, the first projectile may have come up short, while the other two may be over shots. The arrowhead near the Wishart fortification was found in an orientation of 240 degrees, but is believed to be too far from the state monument or pipe marker to be an overshot. Lead balls, many of which are .44 caliber, probably were fired from revolvers in the possession of both sides. Shrapnel could not be identified to caliber, but may indicate areas where lead rounds impacted.

It was hoped the distribution of wagon parts would yield clues to the location of the defense perimeter. Parts should be prevalent if wagon boxes were left in place on the battlefield. Conversely, a lack of parts would be expected if wagons were moved or the area was collected.

Wagon parts actually occur in only two areas (Figure 9, p. 125). The highest concentration is at the Wishart fortification, which suggests that some wagons were left there, whether or not they were the ones involved in the battle (see Spear, 1993:37). The second array is a linear, east-west distribution between the pipe marker locality to the south and the state monument to the north. These artifacts are believed to be near the old pinery road route between the fort and the forest, and the area eventually should be compared to historical maps and infrared aerial photography for evidence of wagon traffic. Dozens of other hardware items, including hooks, nuts, and bolts, were distributed in a nearly identical array as were these 25 wagon parts. Analysts, however, could not confidently identify them as wagon parts so they were not included on the distribution map.

Livestock shoe nails could have been used on horses, mules, or oxen. They were particularly sparse in the pipe marker area, but three apparent groupings are visible in the Sheridan County portion of the project area (Figure 10, 126). The first is a cluster adjacent to the west end of the road leading to the state monument where a modern corral was located. Nails here probably date to the twentieth century. The same may be said for the more dispersed array around the state monument, however some of these may be related to military use in the nineteenth century if reshoeing was conducted at the Wagon Box corral to prepare draft animals for their journey to and from the pineries. The third cluster is at the Wishart fortification that was garrisoned for some time after the Wagon Box Fight; draft animals and riding stock may have been reshod here.

Mule and oxen shoes also are plotted on this map (Figure 10) since both animals are known to have been used as draft animals during the period of the Wagon Box Fight. Horse shoes are not included because investigators were less confident in estimating the antiquity of each specimen. All of the oxen and mule shoes were located either at the Wishart fortification or along the possible remnant of the pinery road. None were found near the pipe marker or state monument.

Another map plots the distribution of cut nails (Figure 11, p. 127), most of which are believed to be contemporary with nineteenth century military use in the area. Several patterns are apparent and each deserves individual consideration. First, there is only one cut nail near the pipe marker, but the area to the north depicts a distribution of cut nails similar to that for wagon parts. A linear, east-west trending pattern follows the northern limit of the survey block that encompasses the pipe marker, and extends into the smaller, trapezoidal block west of the irrigation ditch. This may be the route for the old pinery road. Cut nails could be all that remain from wooden artifacts that became dispersed along the route, or they may have fallen from kegs carrying nails in the back of wagons. Since many of the cut nails were not clenched and actually appeared unused, they easily could have spilled from a storage keg.

A second cluster is seen at the state monument, particularly along the eastern margin of the area, which could be the location of the Wagon Box defense perimeter. A linear dispersal of cut nails between the state monument and the Wishart fortification could indicate the route followed by soldiers if they moved wagons or equipment from the defense site to the new fortification, and nails may have been lost in the process.

Two patterns are visible in the Wishart fortification area. The first is the fortification itself, which contains the highest density of cut nails for any area on the battlefield. The simplest explanation here is that cut nails were associated with the fortification in great numbers, whether they were part of construction activities or were contained in kegs for future use. These items apparently were abandoned at the site when soldiers left, but even their original distribution probably post-dates the Wagon Box Fight by several days. The second pattern is a linear, north-south array that follows an old fence line. Wire staples were found throughout this area as well, but were not retained for curation. On some standing fence posts, two adjacent staples were driven into the wood, horizontal to the ground surface rather than the normal vertical angle, and they were only a centimeter or so apart. This stapling technique is still used on posts in pastures where it becomes necessary to frequently remove the wire and lay it down so it is not destroyed by drifting snow. The wire is stretched between the horizontal staples, rather than stapled to the post, then a third staple or nail is loosely dropped through the opening on each embedded staple to hold the wire against the post. When the wire needs to be laid on the ground, the loose nail is pulled from its position in the staple apertures. If cut nails were abundant at the Wishart fortification, they may have been used in this manner during later fencing operations, explaining their presence in a linear pattern. Alternatively, an old post-and-pole fence may have used cut nails in its construction, but further research is required to determine if one was ever built on this location.

Finally, it was hoped that the soldiers' tent camp might be identified by the distribution of eating utensils lost on the morning of the battle. Once again, however, the most obvious concentration is around the Wishart fortification. There are no eating utensils near the pipe marker to suggest that the tent camp was near there, but fragments of a cup, plate, and bowl were found around the state monument area, suggesting that the state monument is a more likely candidate for the defense perimeter than the pipe marker (Figure 12, p. 128).

A word of caution is warranted when interpreting these artifact distributions—our survey area covered three separate blocks comprising about 40 acres of the battlefield. The entire battlefield is much larger than this and probably covers 1,000 acres. If intervening areas are ever surveyed, the present distribution patterns may take on a whole new relationship to each other. The observations offered here are only possible scenarios. Alternatives cannot be ruled out until the site formation history is better understood.

Summary and Conclusions

The Wagon Box Battlefield

Both the archaeological record and the historical record indicate that the battle of August 2, 1867 took place between Piney Creek and Little Piney Creek about four miles (see p. 47) northwest of Fort Phil Kearny.

This area is a sloping plateau between the Big Horn Mountains to the west and Sullivant Hill to the east. South Piney Creek courses along the northern border of the battlefield and Little Piney Creek along the southern border. While both the state monument in Sheridan County and the pipe marker in Johnson County are integral components of the battlefield landscape, each represents different combat activities.

The principal question addressed in this research is this: where was the Wagon Box corral defense site? An answer cannot be offered with absolute confidence, but a strong argument has been made that the area around the state monument in Sheridan County is a more likely candidate for the defense perimeter than is the pipe marker in Johnson County. The state monument also is closer to key topographic features on the battlefield landscape that were mentioned in the historical record, like the ridge slope about seventy-five yards to the north from which Indian sharpshooters fired at the wagons (Gibson, 1990:58). The most compelling evidence in favor of the state monument, however, comes from the archaeological record.

The Wagon Box corral was adjacent to the infantry camp at the time of the engagement. Consequently, camping gear may have been lost during the melee and entered the archaeological record. Utensils only were found around the state monument area, not the pipe marker. The eating utensils found around the Wishart fortification probably post-date the battle.

Soldier firing positions also were considered. Distinctive .50-70 cartridge cases of the bar anvil type should fall near infantry firing positions along the defense perimeter, since Indian warriors did not have access to this ammunition type during the battle. Previous work by Vaughn, Rickey and others certainly demonstrate the presence of this cartridge case type near the state monument, and most of the cases we found were in this vicinity as well. None were located near the pipe marker in Johnson County.

Iron arrow points and .58 caliber minie balls are expected to represent incoming projectiles fired at the defense perimeter by Native American warriors. Three arrow points were found near the state monument and none near the pipe marker, but .58 caliber slugs were found at both locations. Clearly, both localities are part of the battlefield, but even this evidence supports the former location as the defense site. Iron arrowheads are propelled with much slower velocities than minie balls and are therefore expected to land closer to intended targets when they miss. Muzzleloaders discharging .58 caliber minie balls can propel their bullets several hundred yards beyond the target if they overshoot. Some .58 caliber bullets apparently missed targets near the state monument and carried into the valley of Little Piney Creek.

Projectiles of several kinds should land near target positions from several directions since warriors were armed with a variety of weapons and the Wagon Box defenders were surrounded during the battle. Incoming projectiles near the state monument suggest multiple trajectories by different missile types and therefore support its status as the defense perimeter.

Initially, wagon parts and associated metal objects were expected at the true defense site, however this research has revealed a lack of wagon parts at both the state monument and pipe marker. Even so, a subtle, linear dispersal of cut nails between the state monument and the Wishart fortification may have resulted from wagon parts or spilled nails lost during removal of wagon boxes after the battle. Although wagon parts were not found at either the state monument or the pipe marker, this linear array may support the state monument area as the site of the Wagon Box corral since it might be the source of items that later became dispersed on their way to the Wishart fortification.

Finally, historical records argue that the battle was fought by hundreds of combatants for at least four hours. Repeated charges were staged and many guns were constantly fired. Archaeologists expect this type of intense activity to generate a high density of combat debris. Although the battlefield has been combed by collectors for many years, a quantifiable record should remain. Comparatively speaking, this research has shown that period artifacts are far more frequent near the state monument than the pipe marker. In fact, most of the material in the pipe marker vicinity probably post-dates the battle.

Although our research indicates that the state monument in Sheridan County is a more likely candidate for the Wagon Box corral than is the pipe marker in Johnson County, both locations are clearly part of the overall battlefield landscape. Our research did not address any other possible location for the corral, because we were limited to the survey block parameters. The Wishart fortification is documented well enough historically and archaeologically (now), so it was not a candidate. It is important to remember that we only surveyed 40 acres or so of a battlefield that probably covers at least 1,000 acres (about a 4% sample). This is a very small portion of the potential archaeological record.

Since the vegetation was thick, bent over and blanketed the ground in many places, the accuracy and precision of metal detection transects were limited. Future transects run over the same ground in a pattern perpendicular to transects in this study, and after the forage has been removed, almost certainly would produce additional evidence. The use of metal detectors, however, imparts a bias toward the discovery of metallic artifacts and items either attached to metal parts or within the bounds of the small excavations that unearthed metallic objects. Numerous non-metallic artifacts and features, such as stone arrow points or fire hearths, may still be present.

The Battlefield Pattern Model

Archaeologists successfully outlined one Indian Wars battlefield scenario with a distinctive archaeological signature when they focused on the June 25, 1876 engagement between five companies of the Seventh U. S. Cavalry and a force of Sioux and Cheyenne warriors on the Little Bighorn River in Montana (Fox and Scott, 1991; Fox, 1993; Scott and Fox, 1987; Scott, et. al., 1989). Contrary to some historical accounts, these researchers argue the engagement contained episodes of tactical stability, followed by disintegration and chaos. Artifact distributions suggest that Native Americans infiltrated commanding positions on the battlefield and fired at close range into the army ranks using repeating weapons — a much more useful firearm for close in-fighting than the single shot Springfield breech loaders used by the troopers.

This battlefield pattern reveals a landscape where Native American warriors and cavalry units held numerous firing positions throughout the engagement. Native American positions increased in number through time and moved across the battlefield toward an ever narrowing perimeter within which the cavalry became trapped. As the front collapsed toward Last Stand Hill, Native American positions overtook ground only recently held by troopers, generating a pattern of overlapping battlefield debris. Items also became dispersed as Native Americans gathered the spoils of war after they killed all of the soldiers.

The Little Bighorn scenario provides a glimpse of one type of battlefield pattern produced by combat during the Indian Wars. Others may occur depending on several variables, and each pattern would reflect differences in the archaeological record (Miller et. al., 1997). Important variables include weapons technology, the number and arrangement of firing positions, the number and arrangement of target positions, and the marksmanship of combatants. All of these variables can change horizontally across a battlefield and temporally as sequential episodes of a battle unfold. Resulting configurations can be influenced by terrain, tactical shifts, military branch (e.g., cavalry or infantry), duration of engagement, and involvement of noncombatants, to name just a few. Archaeological recognition of these factors allows investigators to model different battlefield patterns. The Wagon Box Fight is an example of a battlefield pattern where a single defensive position was maintained throughout the engagement, in contrast to the tactical disintegration at the Little Bighorn.

Archaeological research reveals considerable variability in distribution patterns of combat related artifacts on Indian Wars battlefields. The archaeological evidence for different types of engagements, however, needs to be quantified for the post-Civil War battlefield pattern to survive as a robust, analytical model. Since Fox and Scott's (1991) work stimulated new thinking on military sites archaeology, archaeologists now must be more aware of the potential for problem-oriented fieldwork opportunities and the need to properly evaluate variables that influence formation histories of the archaeological record. Fox and Scott (1991:102) called for comparative data to develop an Indian Wars pattern on the frontier and the archaeological record at the Wagon Box Fight helps bring us closer to this goal.

Acknowledgments

The 1993-1994 archaeological investigations at the Wagon Box Fight site (48SH129) could not have been accomplished without the assistance and enthusiasm of several individuals and groups. They have provided an enormous contribution to the history of Wyoming, as well as educational benefits to present and future generations who share an interest in our western heritage.

The Fort Phil Kearny/Bozeman Trail Association (FPK/BTA) supported the project both financially and logistically. They also coordinated the volunteer program, handled press releases, and promoted the project. Mary Ellen McWilliams, Katie Curtiss, and Cindy Perciful deserve special recognition in this capacity.

Wyoming State Parks and Historic Sites (SPHS) staff at Fort Phil Kearny were particularly helpful. Sonny Reisch, Bob Wilson, and Linda DeTavernier provided communications, equipment storage and use, interpretive tours, historical research, and facilities access. The staff also served as liaison with landowners, arranged access to private lands within the battlefield area, and responded to numerous public inquiries about the project. Our thanks for all you did.

Special thanks go to the Wuthier family for allowing us access to their property. Their gracious permission enabled us to investigate the pipe marker location and areas adjacent to the Wishart fortification. Their careful management of the area has helped protect the archaeological site for research and interpretation.

People came from all over the country to help with these investigations, including California, Colorado, Florida, Montana, Pennsylvania, Washington, Wisconsin, Wyoming, and British Columbia. Volunteers for the 1993 season included Carolyn and Jim Buff, William (Bill) Daley, Jane Decker, John DeMay, Jerry Forwood, Rich Gilbert, Don Hefferman, Sherri Hickman, Dennis Irvin, Charles J. Kavalec, John Kuzara, Diane Marsden, Dean O'Connor, Carl Oslund, Jim Powers, Ed Smyth, James (Jim) H. C. Walker, and Roger Wardlow. In 1994, the volunteers included Gil Bullock, Rich and Inge Coates, Julie Coleman-Fike, Bill Daley, John DeMay, B. J. Earle, Sterling Fenn, Don Hefferman, Dean O'Connor, Kevin O'Dell, Jim Powers, Ed Remeika, Jr., and Don and Bobbie Woerner. The field crews endured snow, rain, cold, heat, wind, lightning strikes, and long, often tedious days.

Laboratory analysis was ably supported by the efforts of Judith A. Brown, curator for the Office of the Wyoming State Archaeologist. Thanks also go to Tom Lindmier, Superintendent of South Pass City State Historic Site, who helped identify wagon parts collected from the project area. His knowledge, expertise, and library added greatly to this study. Sterling Fenn provided valuable insights during the analysis of cartridges and their components.

These people energized the quest to recover more information about the battle that took place above Fort Phil Kearny over 130 years ago. Their commitment proves once again that cooperative efforts can produce substantive research. Our since gratitude to everyone mentioned here and to those who may have been inadvertently omitted.

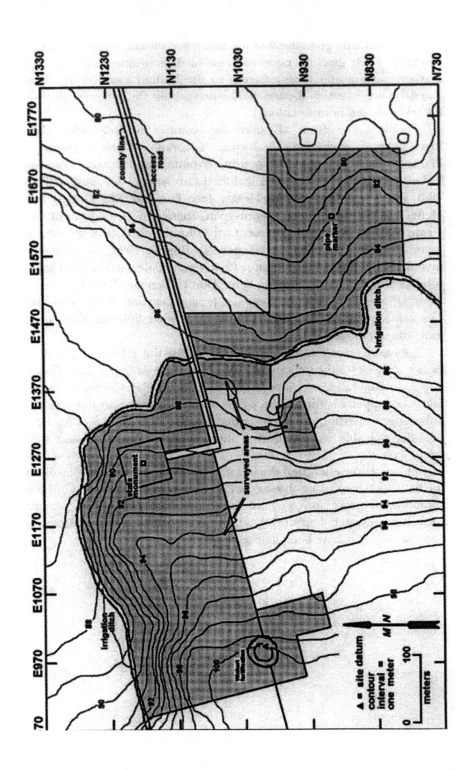

Examples of .50-.70 Springfield cartridge cases recovered from the site of The Wagon Box Fight.

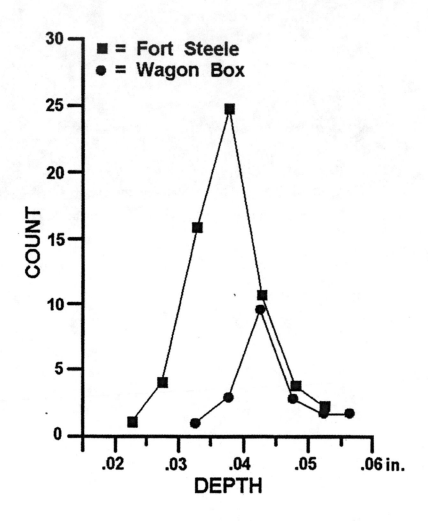

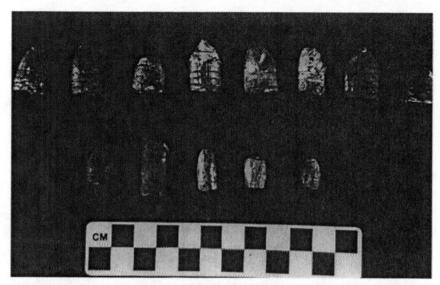

Examples of conical bullets. Top row, second, fourth, and fifth from right are .58 caliber. Top row, far right, is the .58 caliber that may have been cut.

Metal arrowheads.

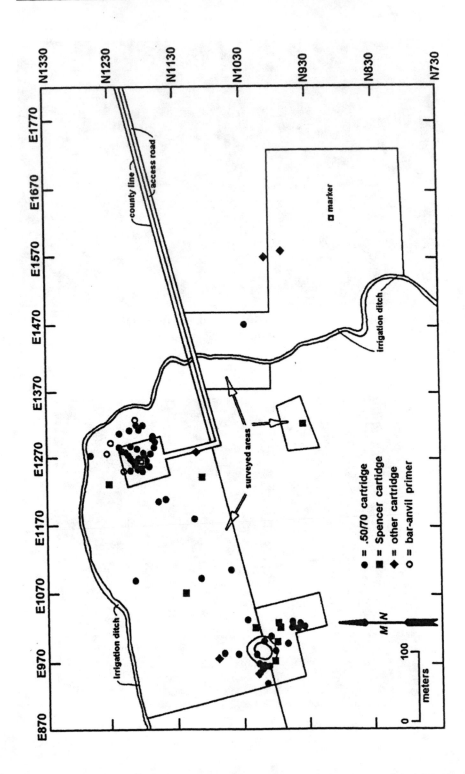

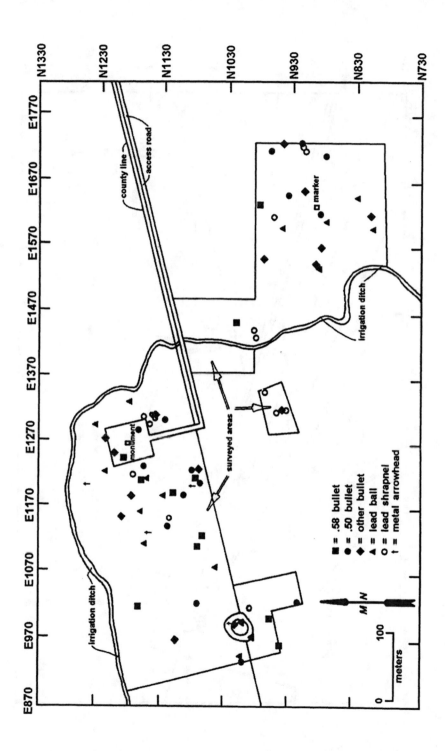

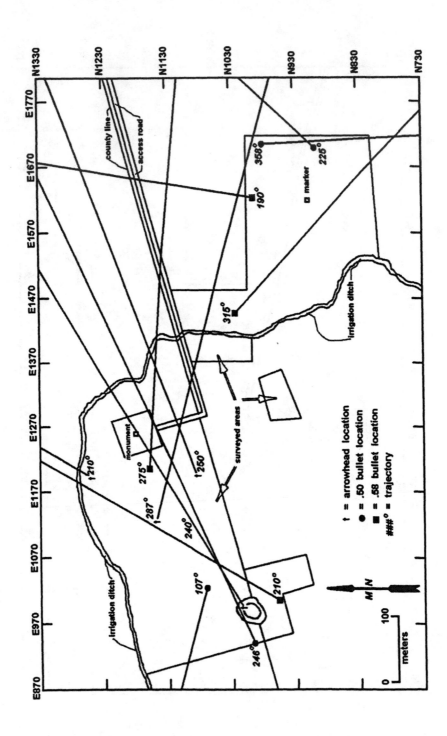

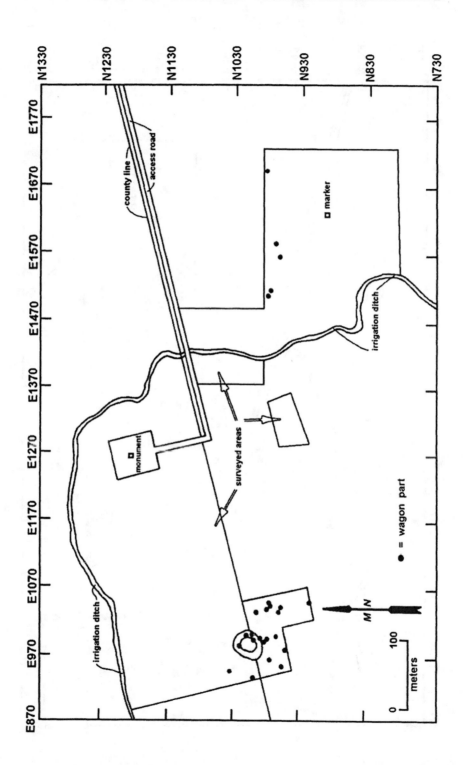

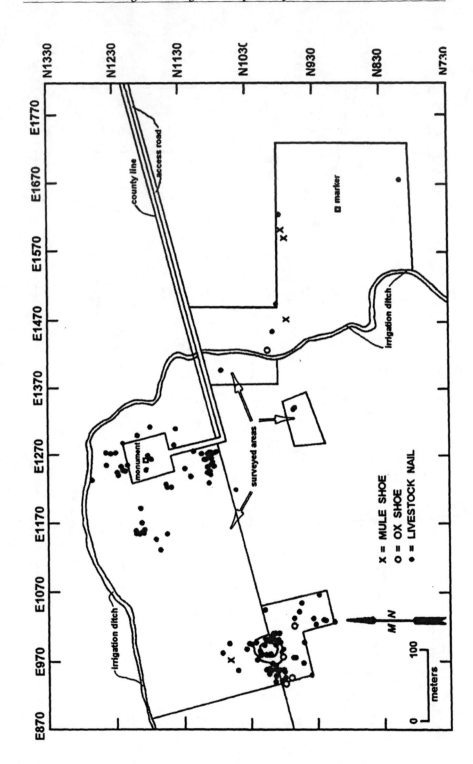

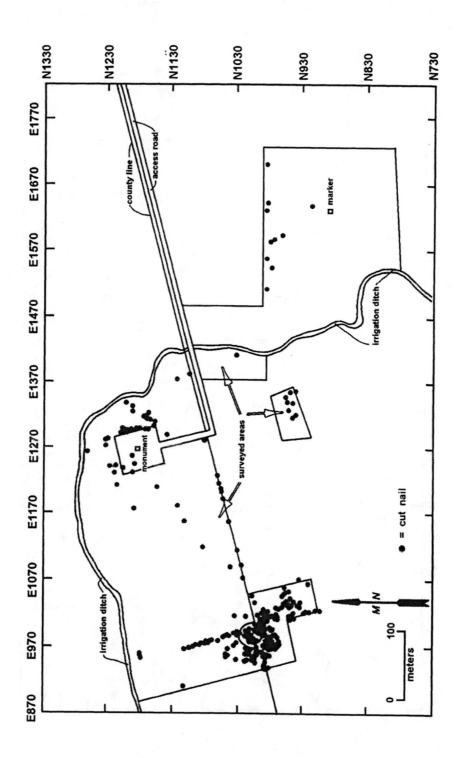

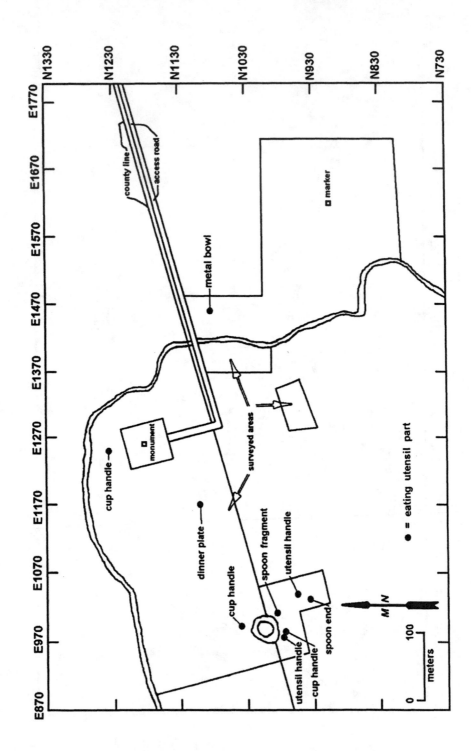

Notes

1. Murray, *Military Posts*, pp. 6-8; Hebard/Brininstool, *The Bozeman Trail*, Vol. 1, pp. 205-220; Doyle, "The Bozeman Trail, 1863-1868," *Annals of Wyoming*, Vol. 70, No. 2, Spring 1998. There was also some overland traffic from the Minnesota area.

2. In addition to the "Bozeman Road" or "Trail," the route was variously called "The Montana Road," "Big Horn Road," "Virginia City Road," and "Powder River Road" among others. Of these, the "Bozeman Trail" was the most widely used designation. See Doyle, "The Bozeman Trail, 1863-1868," *Annals of Wyoming*; Hebard and Brininstool, *The Bozeman Trail*, Vol. 1, pp. 213-214.

3. Doyle, "The Bozeman Trail, 1863-1868" *Annals of Wyoming*, pp. 3-1.

4. Lowe, "The Bridger Trail," *Annals of Wyoming*, pp. 12-23; Doyle, "The Bozeman Trail, *Annals of Wyoming*, pp. 10-11; Murray, *Military Posts*, p.7; Hebard/Brininstool, *The Bozeman Trail*, Vol. 1, p. 219.

5. Murray, *Military Posts*, pp. 11-12; Carrington, *Absaraka*, p. 38.

6. Murray, *Army on the Powder River*, pp. 2-3; Magruder, Theodore, "Colonel Henry Beebe Carrington," *Portraits of Fort Phil Kearny*, pp. 16-20.

7. The Nebraska post was named for Gen. Stephen Watts Kearny of Mexican War fame, while the later Fort Phil Kearny was named for Gen. Philip Kearny, killed at the Battle of Chantilly, Virginia in the Civil War. See Carrington, *My Army Life*, p.xi. During the period of its existence, those stationed at the fort spelled Kearny with an "e," thus Fort Kearney, despite the spelling of the man for whom the post was named. "Kearny" did not become the official spelling until many years later. See Carrington, *My Army Life*, Introduction by John D. McDermott, p. xi.

8. Hebard/Brininstool, *The Bozeman Trail*, Vol. 1, pp. 268, 294; Carrington, *Absaraka*, pp. 41-42; Utley, *Frontier Regulars*, p.102. During his tenure at Fort Phil Kearny, Carrington's wife was Margaret Irvin McDowell Carrington, who later wrote *Absaraka: Home of the Crows*. After Margaret's death from tuberculosis in 1870, Carrington married Francis Grummond, whose husband, George had been killed in the Fetterman disaster. Francis also wrote of her experiences at Fort Phil Kearny in a volume entitled *My Army Life*.

9. Hebard/Brininstool, *The Bozeman Trail*, Vol. I, pp. 267-268; Carrington, *Absaraka*, p. 79; Utley, *Frontier Regulars*, pp. 102-103; Larson, *Red Cloud*, pp.

90-94. A popular image of Red Cloud's reaction upon seeing Carrington and his troops was to remark that "The Great Father sends us presents and wants us to sell him the road, but White Chief goes with soldiers to steal the road before the Indians say Yes or No." See Carrington, *My Army Life*, pp. 46-47, and Utley, *Frontier Regulars*, p. 103. Whether Red Cloud actually expressed his reaction in these words is, in my opinion, questionable, although it undoubtedly reflected his true feelings on the matter. See Larson, *Red Cloud*, pp. 92-93.

10. Murray, *Military Posts*, pp. 19-21; Utley, *Frontier Regulars*, p. 104.

11. Murray, *Military Posts*, pp. 38, 43.

12. The actual straight-line distance from the fort to the wagon box corral is about four miles. However, the over-the-ground distance is closer to five miles, or even a bit farther depending on the precise points of measurement.

13. Hebard/Brininstool, *The Bozeman Trail*, Vol. II, p. 93. Today Piney Island is the site of Story, Wyoming. During the 1860s, the area was mistakenly referred to as "Piney Island" due to an error in mapping. See *Piney Island: A Guide to the Story Area*, p. 24.

14. *Piney Island*, pp. 29, 31; Murray, *Army on the Powder River*, p. 8.

15. Murray, *Military Posts*, p. 74; Utley, *Frontier Regulars*, pp. 105-106.

16. Utley, *Frontier Regulars*, pp. 104,107.

17. Murray, *Military Posts*, p. 79.

18. Perhaps the best example of the potential danger awaiting the solitary traveler is that of Ridgway Glover a reporter and photographer in the employ of *Frank Leslie's Illustrated Weekly* whose scalped and mutilated corpse was found some two miles from the fort, following a solitary junket into the mountains. See Hagan "Ridgway Glover," *Portraits of Fort Phil Kearny*, pp. 39-41. Glover has also been described as an "artist" and reporter. See Hebard/Brininstool, *The Bozeman Trail*, Vol. II, p. 282.

19. Hebard/Brininstool, *The Bozeman Trail*, Vol. II, p. 93. Pilot Knob was variously called Picket Hill, Pilot Hill, or Pilot Knob.

20. The name Sullivant Hills honored the family of Colonel Carrington's first wife, Margaret Irvin McDowell Sullivant.

21. Hebard/Brininstool, *The Bozeman Trail*, Vol. I, p. 293; Carrington, *Absaraka*, pp. 138-139. Fessenden claims that twenty wagons were sent out from the fort each morning, but whether this means two trains of ten wagons each is not made clear. See Hebard/Brininstool, *The Bozeman Trail*, Vol. II, p. 93.

22. Hebard/Brininstool, *The Bozeman Trail*, Vol. II, p. 93.

23. Accounts differ as to the number of blockhouses that were built. Robert Murray says three blockhouses were constructed at the Pinery. However, F. M. Fessenden, a member of the Fort Phil Kearny garrison, says that one blockhouse was built at each ("cutting") pinery. See Murray, *Military Posts*, p. 47 and Hebard/Brininstool, *The Bozeman Trail*, Vol. II, p.93. Neither is it clear as to whether these were actual blockhouses, though that seems unlikely. They may have been little more than a defensive enclosure from which guards could fire on

attacking Indians. Murray also says they were built and manned by the wood cutters. Murray, *Military Posts*, p. 47.

24. *Ibid.*, p. 80; Utley, *Frontier Regulars*, p. 107. Utley has pointed out that Fort Laramie, far to the south and out of harm's way, had a garrison nearly twice as large as that of Fort Phil Kearny.

25. Murray, *Military Posts*, pp. 68-69; Utley, *Frontier Regulars*, p. 107.

26. Murray, *Military Posts*, pp. 80-82; Utley, *Frontier Regulars*, p. 106.

27. Murray, *Military Posts*, pp. 11-12; Utley, *Frontier Regulars*, pp. 106-107.

28. Utley, *Frontier Regulars*, p. 107.

29. There is some disagreement as to the number of Indians involved. Robert Murray (*Military Posts*, pp. 82-83) believed there were about 300. Robert Utley (*Frontier Regulars*, pp. 107-108) says 100, while Margaret Carrington, writing in *Absaraka* (pp. 104-107) claims 200.

30. Strictly speaking, Carrington could have refused Fetterman's request, but the army's system of seniority carried much weight. It is also very possible that Carrington went along with the request in the belief that it would have helped shore-up the weak relationship with his staff.

31. It should be pointed out that there is a fundamental difference between breech-loading weapons such as the Spencer and so-called repeaters such as the Henry and its successor, the Winchester. Operating a breech-loader is a two-step procedure: first, operating the lever-action either feeds a fresh cartridge into the chamber from a magazine (e.g., Spencer), or opens the breech to allow the cartridge to be inserted manually (e.g., Sharps). Second, the hammer must then be manually cocked before the weapon may be fired. By contrast, the Henry or Winchester employs a one-step procedure, wherein operating the lever-action feeds a fresh shell into the chamber and automatically cocks the weapon at the same time. In both systems, operating the lever-action also ejects the spent cartridge from the chamber.

32. *Ibid.*, pp. 108-109; Hebard, *The Bozeman Trail*, Vol. 1, pp. 303-305; Carrington, *My Army Life*, p. 143. For one argument challenging the position that Fetterman was entirely at fault, see Vaughn, *Indian Fights*, pp. 24-28.

33. Murray, *Military Posts*, p. 83.

34. Utley, *Frontier Regulars*, pp. 109-110; Murray, *Military Posts*, p. 83.

35. Sandoz, *Crazy Horse*, p. 199; James C. Olson, *Red Cloud and the Sioux Problem*, pp. 51, 76. Larson, *Red Cloud*, pp. 101-106.

36. The ride of Portugee Phillips became one of the enduring myths of the Old West. Like most myths, its core story is true, but it has suffered from considerable embellishment. See Murray, *The Bozeman Trail*, pp. 48-49; Murray, *The Army on the Powder River*, pp. 11-26.

37. Murray, *Military Posts*, pp. 86-87.

38. Carrington, *Absaraka*, p. 227. Actually, a detachment of twenty men under the new acting quartermaster, Captain George B. Dandy arrived from Fort C.F. Smith on 27 December, preceding the Wessells column by nearly a month. See Murray, *Military Posts*, p. 86.

39. Utley, *Frontier Regulars*, pp. 12, 102; Murray, *Military Posts*, pp. 84-86; Weigley, *History of the U.S. Army*, p. 266; Murray, *The Army on the Powder River*, pp. 8-9.

40. Murray, *Military Posts*, pp. 85-86.

41. The late Stanley Vestal was of the opinion that only the Battle of the Little Bighorn has received more attention than the Wagon Box Fight. Vestal, *Warpath*, p. 70. John Hunton, a long time resident of the Fort Laramie area and who was employed in the sutler's store said that the Wagon Box Fight was a popular topic of conversation for some two years. See Hunton to Reckmeyer, March 23, 1927.

42. Reckmeyer, *"The Truth About The Wagon Box Fight,"* p. 1. Dodge, *33 Years Among Our Wild Indians*, Dunn, *Massacres of the Mountains*, pp. 500-506, and Brady *Indian Fights and Fighters*, pp. 40-58; Hebard/Brininstool, *The Bozeman Trail*, Vol. II, pp. 70-71, 80.

43. Murray, *Military Posts*, p. 87.

44. *Ibid.*, pp. 92-93; Heitman, *Historical Register*, pp. 894, 900.

45. Murray, *Military Posts*, pp. 92-93; Hebard/Brininstool, *The Bozeman Trail*, Vol.II, pp. 40-43.

46. Murray, *Military Posts*, p.67; *U.S.A. Ordinance Department Manual*; Hammer, *The Springfield Carbine* p. 1; Lord, *The Civil War Collector's Encyclopedia*, pp. 237-243.

47. Hammer, *The Springfield Carbine*, p. 1; Letter, Sterling Fenn to Author, Feb. 1990.

48. Murray, *Military Posts*, p. 93, Fenn to Author, Feb. 1990.

49. Murray, *Military Posts*, pp. 92-93. Post Returns, Fort Philip Kearny, D.T., August 1, 1867. Fort Kearny never had more than a few pieces of artillery, so that reference to 38 guns would have to mean mostly rifles and perhaps a few sidearms in addition to those field pieces the post did have.

50. *Ibid.*, pp. 94-95.

51. Schrebeis, "The Wagon Box Fight," *Old Travois Trails*, Vol. III, May-June 1942, p. 7.

52. *Ibid.*, p. 7; Hebard/Brininstool, *The Bozeman Trail*, Vol. II, p. 43.

53. Hebard/Brininstool, p. 43; Schreibeis, "The Wagon Box Fight," p. 7;William Murphy, who was stationed at Fort Phil Kearny at the time, but who was not in the fight says that the wagons were only able to haul a few logs at a time from the "pinery" to the corral. The logs were dumped in a pile fifteen to twenty feet from the corral. The running gear of the wagons was then loaded to full capacity from this supply for the final stage of the journey to Fort Kearny. See Murphy, William, "The Forgotten Battalion," *Annals of Wyoming*, Vol. VI & VII, July -October 1929.

54. Sam Gibson stated that the wagons were the same kind as those used in the Civil War. Frederic Claus, another participant described them as being of the common prairie schooner variety. Hebard/Brininstool, *The Bozeman Trail*, Vol. II, pp. 43-44, 50-51, 84. William Murphy said the sides of the boxes were about five feet high. "The Forgotten Battalion," *Annals of Wyoming*, Vol. VI & VII,

July-October 1929, p. 394; See also, Schreibeis, "The Wagon Box Fight," p. 7. Since the army provided the wagons, they would have to have been government issue, which would make them the M-1861, 6-mule U.S. Army QM Wagon. And since the boxes measured 10' X 4.5' X 2.5' high, it seems reasonable to conclude that 14 such boxes laid end-to-end would result in a corral approximately 60-70' long X 25-30' wide. H. Sterling Fenn, Comments to author, 2-4-90. Gibson, however, said the corral was 120' long X 70' wide (*The Denver Post,* August 1, 1919), while Littman remembered the corral as being 80' long X 50' wide, Hebard, "Marking The Oregon Trail, The Bozeman Road and Historic Places in Wyoming, 1908-1920," The DAR, p. 42. One of the defenders, Ashton P. Barton claimed that the boxes were raised a foot off the ground and that some men were positioned underneath them. See Masters to Hebard, June 23, 1926.

55. Captain James Powell, Letter to Adjutant, Fort Phil Kearny, August 4, 1867. Understanding the importance of the role "visual control" played in selecting the location of the wagon box corral is essential to any study that attempts to verify the correct site.

56. Hebard/Brininstool, *The Bozeman Trail*, Vol. 11, pp. 44, 59, 62-63. Gibson's description is at odds with the sketch he furnished E.A. Brininstool in which two complete wagons are shown to the immediate west of the corral and one wagon box with canvas top as part of the west wall of the corral. See Hebard/Brininstool, *The Bozeman Trail*, Vol. II, p. 55.

57. Colonel Richard Irving Dodge probably laid the foundation for this misconception in his *33 Years Among Our Wild Indians*, p. 481, first published in 1882. The story was repeated in Jacob Dunn, *Massacres of the Mountains* p. 430, published in 1886, and again, in George A. Forsyth, *The Story of a Soldier*, p. 191, which appeared in 1900. In his *Indian Fights and Fighters* (pp. 43-44), C.T. Brady rejects the allegation, but does point out that nearly every writer up to that time claimed the wagon boxes were lined with iron. Interestingly, one source that does support the story of metal-lined wagon boxes is that of a man named O.M. Osborn, who apparently was an employee of the wood contractor on that day. Osborn repeatedly told Doane Robinson that the boxes were indeed lined with iron. See Doane Robinson to Mrs. C.S. Paine, Librarian, State Historical Society of Nebraska, January 26, 1923. Found in B.J. Hagan Collection, Sheridan , Wyoming Public Library (Hereafter cited as Hagan Coll.). For accounts stating that this had no basis in fact, see Hebard/Brininstool, The Bozeman Trail, Vol. II, pp. 50-51, 75, 84-85; C.T. Brady, Indian Fights and Fighters, p. 66. Letter from General David S. Gordon to General A.E. Bates, February 9, 1908, found in Hagan Coll. Roy Appleman's account of the battle in *Great Western Indian Fights*, p. 150, suggests that some of the boxes may have had loopholes but this, too, has been denied by both Sam Gibson and Max Littman, although William Murphy told Grace Raymond Hebard that the wagons did have loopholes. See E. A. Brininstool to Grace R. Hebard, September 11, 1919. Hebard Coll., Western American Heritage Center, University of Wyoming, Laramie. C.T. Brady claims that there were augurs in the corral and

that Powell's men used them to bore holes in the sides of the wagon boxes. See Brady, *Indian Fights*, p. 44.

58. Hebard/ Brininstool, *The Bozeman Trail*, Vol. II, p. 43; Murray, *Military Posts*, p.94-95; Hyde, *Red Cloud's Folk*, pp. 158-159. Larson, *Red Cloud*, p. 110. Finn Burnett's biographer claims that Red Cloud had a disagreement with the Miniconjous over their destination and that they wound up going to Fort C.F. Smith, while Red Cloud headed for Fort Phil Kearny, got sidetracked by the wood train and was defeated. See David, *Finn Burnett, Frontiersman*, p. 194.

59. It is not clear as to which Little Wolf was in the Wagon Box Fight. According to Willis Rowland, an interpreter at the Lame Deer Agency, the Cheyenne contingent was under "the older Chief Little Wolf." George Bird Grinnell, however, refers to "Young Little Wolf," sometimes called Laban Little Wolf, and a son of the "older Little Wolf." See "News Release from Richard Randolph, Lame Deer, Montana, 18 April, 1927," in Hagan Coll.

60. Robert Larson's biography conveys the impression that Red Cloud was present. See Larson, *Red Cloud*, pp. 112-114, 158-159, 289. In *Red Cloud and the Sioux Problem* (pp. 64-65), James C. Olson also suggests Red Cloud was on hand. According to Stanley Vestal, the principal chief present was "Flying By." Red Cloud reportedly was present but did not exercise any authority. The attack on the wagon box corral was obviously not intended as a quick hit-and-run strike, but an event of some importance, as is evidenced by the size of the attacking party. In view of this it does seems likely that Red Cloud would have been on the scene. As with the number of Indians in the war party and the number of casualties, efforts to identify the principal Indian leaders is nearly hopeless. In addition to the above, for example, in 1918, Big Bat Pourier told Walter Camp that One Bear was the Sioux chief; that Red Cloud was not on hand. Black Horse told Camp that Sitting Bull and Dull Knife were both present. See Camp Field Notes, Envelope 71, Lilly Library, Indiana University, Bloomington, Indiana.

61. Estimates as to the size of the attacking force vary greatly. George Bird Grinnell believed there were only 300 Sioux and 75-100 Cheyennes. The estimate of Cheyennes is substantiated by Willis Rowland a government interpreter at the Lame Deer Agency who got the figure from the Cheyennes. See "News Release From Richard Randolph, Lame Deer, Montana, April 18, 1927," found in Hagan Coll. Vestal and Hyde agree that the force numbered about 1000, while C.T. Brady put the number at 3000. Robert Larson says the force was mainly Oglalas and numbered 800-1000. See Larson, Red Cloud, p. 111; George Bird Grinnell, "The Wagon Box Fight," *Midwest Review*, Vol. IX, Feb-March 1928, p. 5; Hyde, *Red Cloud's Folk*, 159; Vestal, *Warpath*, pp. 71-72; Olson, *Red Cloud and the Sioux Problem*, pp. 64-65; Brady, *Indian Fights and Fighters*, p. 48. Littman thought the attackers did not exceed 2,000 in number, though he believed there may have been as many as 3,000 between the corral and the fort. See Littman to Camp, August 22, 1919. Jim Bridger arrived at Fort Kearny from Fort C.F. Smith several days after the fight and reportedly declared that the Indian tail was the biggest he'd ever seen,

though it is always well to keep in mind Bridger's fondness for embellishment See, Letter, W.N. Magill to Walter Camp, February 26, 1917.

62. Hyde, *Red Cloud's Folk*, p. 159; Grinnell, "The Wagon Box Fight," p. 6.

63. Powell, Letter to Adjutant, Fort Phil Kearny, August 4, 1867; Special Order #128, Hdq., Fort Phil Kearny, July 31, 1867. Copy in Robert A. Murray Collection, Wyoming Room, Sheridan County, Wyoming Fulmer Public Library (Hereafter cited as Murray Collection); Sam Gibson recalled that the wagons were packed with supplies for a month, but the official order specified ten days. Hebard/Brininstool, *The Bozeman Trail*, Vol. II, pp. 43-44.

64. Heitman, *Historical Register and Dictionary of the United States Army*, Vol. I, p.802; Murray, *Military Posts*, p. 51. Fenn, "Captain James Powell," *Portraits of Fort Phil Kearny*, pp. 203-209.

65. Powell, "Pension File, Certificate 573451," RG 15, National Archives; Straight, Michael, "The Strange Testimony of Major Powell," *New York Westerners Brand Book*, Vol. VII, 1960. Fenn, "Captain James Powell," *Portraits of Fort Phil Kearny*, p.208. With one exception, Powell's conduct during the Wagon Box Fight has never, to my knowledge, been subjected to criticism or condemnation. However, in his account of the fight, author T. C. Diers claims that after returning to the corral from the creek where he had been bathing, Powell, overcome and exhausted, lay on the ground "sick and vomiting the entire morning." See Diers, "The Wagon Box Fight," *The Prairie Schooner*, Vol. 2, No. 3, 1928. Where Diers got his information from is unknown, since the article lacks citations. Moreover, other suspect statements render the Diers version of the fight a questionable account at any rate.

66. Heitman, *Historical Register*, Vol. 1, p. 572; Brady, *Indian Fights and Fighters*, p.67; McChristian, Douglas C., "Lieutenant John C. Jenness "A Gallant & Promising Young Officer," *Portraits of Fort Phil Kearny*, pp. 213-217.

67. Powell to Adjutant Fort Phil Kearny, August 4, 1867. John I. Minnich, one of the civilian employees at the side camp, recalled that their camp was on the south side of Little Piney Creek, about 100 rods from the corral, or approximately 183 yards. If one assumes that the large marker represents the approximate site of the corral, then this estimate is in error because it is at least 1/2 mile from the marker to Little Piney Creek. Moreover, Gibson's picket post was some 400 yards from the corral and the side camp was another 4-500 yards beyond that point.

68. Powell, Letter to Adjutant, Fort Phil Kearny, August 4, 1867; Appleman, "The Wagon Box Fight," p. 149; George Geier, "The Side Camp," *Old Travois Trails*, Vol.11, July-August 1941, p. 14. South Piney Creek is sometimes referred to as Big Piney and is located north of the site of the wagon box corral, while Little Piney is to the south. Appleman says the wood cutting camp was across Big Piney, but Powell's report says Little Piney, and Gibson described all of the action as taking place at the "lower pinery," which was across Little Piney Creek. See also Hebard/Brininstool, *The Bozeman Trail*, Vol. II, pp. 43-45. Evidently, there was no logging operation at the Upper Pinery at this time.

69. William Murphy to Walter Camp, April 3, 1917; Hebard/Brininstool, *The Bozeman Trail*, Vol. II, p. 45. One wonders whether Jess was also in the corral during the fight. Perhaps he returned to the fort with the wood train? I have seen no further reference to the animal in any other account. According to Sam Gibson, Jack McDonough was a member of the escort that went to the lower pinery and Jess probably went along, but we have no idea as to whether he eventually made it back to the fort.

70. Hebard/Brininstool, *The Bozeman Trail,* Vol. II, pp. 45-47.

71. One account claims that Powell was accompanied by two others, but does not identify them. See Diers, "The Wagon Box Fight," pp. 196.

72. Lance-corporal is a British army term. A private was assigned as lance-corporal on a temporary basis.

73. Twenty-seventh Regiment of Infantry, "Descriptive Books," National Archives, RG 393, p. 50; Letter D.B. Bradford to Gibson, May 1, 1923.

74. *Ibid.,* pp. 46, 73, 83; Fenn, Comments to author, 2-4-90; Hebard/Brininstool, *The Bozeman Trail,* Vol. II, p. 46.

75. Brady, *Indian Fights and Fighters,* p. 66.

76. Hebard/Brininstool, *The Bozeman Trail,* Vol. II, pp. 46-47; Gibson, who claimed the bullet ricocheted off a rock, must have been blest with truly remarkable eyesight to observe the strike of a bullet on a rock seven hundred yards away. Gibson's comment about not having had an opportunity to test his new rifle supports the claim that there had been no target practice prior to the Wagon Box Fight. See Murray, *Military Posts,* p. 94.

77. *Ibid.,* p. 47.

78. Geier, "The Side Camp," p. l4; Letter, William Murphy to Walter Camp, April 3, 1917.

79. Geier, "The Side Camp," p. l5.

80. *Ibid.,* pp. l5-16. Crazy Horse reportedly led this strike against the side camp and pursued the fleeing wood cutters, but was forced to do so alone because his comrades were more interested in scalps and plunder. When Crazy Horse returned, he found them eating molasses and bread left behind by the wood cutters. See Sandoz, *Crazy Horse,* p. 212.

81. Hebard/Brininstool, *The Bozeman Trail,* Vol. II, pp. 48-49. Again, one must question Sam Gibson's eyesight. The Indian may very well have been carrying a Spencer, perhaps captured from one of Fetterman's cavalrymen, but it seems to me he would have to have been awfully close in order for Gibson to identify the weapon.

82. Hebard and Brininstool,*The Bozeman Trail,* Vol. II, pp. 48-49.

83. Hebard/Brininstool, *The Bozeman Trail,* Vol. II, pp. 49, 73; Enlistment File, Max Littman, AGO File, Record Group 393, National Archives; Keenan, Jerry, "Max Littman: Immigrant Soldier in the Wagon Box Fight," pp. 1-2; author unknown, "The Wagon Box Fight," p. 14.

84. Hebard/Brininstool, *The Bozeman Trail,* Vol. II, pp. 50, 73, 83-84.

85. Powell, Letter to Adjutant, Fort Phil Kearny, August 4, 1867. Sam Gibson claimed that the fight began about seven a.m., and C.T. Brady says that some years after the fight Powell also said seven a.m. Brady, *Indian Fights and Fighters*, p. 46. Powell, Letter to Adjutant, Fort Phil Kearny, August 4, 1867. Max Littman also said 7:00 a.m. See Camp Notes, Wagon Box Fight, Hagan Coll.

86. The only source for this statement is Brady, *Indian Fights and Fighters*, p. 47. It seems reasonable that Powell might have employed such a maneuver, but if so, why did he not mention it in his official report? See Powell, Letter to Adjutant, Fort Phil Kearny, August 4, 1867. It is unclear whether the wood train managed to return to the fort, or if the escort and civilian members of the train were compelled to abandon it and also seek sanctuary in the mountains. In his official report, Major Benjamin Smith who commanded the relief column says only that some returned to the fort. See Smith to Adjutant, Ft. Phil Kearny, August 3, 1867.

87. Powell, Letter to Adjutant, Fort Phil Kearny, August 4, 1867.

88. Brady, *Indian Fights and Fighters*, pp. 50 73; Hebard/Brininstool, *The Bozeman Trail*, Vol. II, pp. 51-53.

89. Hebard/Brininstool, *The Bozeman Trail*, Vol. II, pp. 51-53. One account says that Private Doyle had these extra weapons, plus a Prussian needle gun. Koster, *The Wagon Box Fight*, p. 33. It seems far more likely, however, that a civilian such as Smyth would have had additional weapons, and indeed, Smyth's own account makes this claim. See Brady, *Indian Fights and Fighters*, p. 67.

90. Although Red Cloud may well have been there, it is doubtful that Jenness would have recognized him. More likely, he noted an Indian who perhaps seemed to be in command and assumed it was Red Cloud. See Camp Notes on Wagon Box Fight, Hagan Coll.

91. Powell, Letter to Adjutant, Fort Phil Kearny, August 4, 1867.

92. Powell, Letter to Adjutant, Fort Phil Kearny, August 4, 1867; Hebard/Brininstool, *The Bozeman Trail*, Vol. 11, pp. 53-54, 76. Sterling Fenn who has done much Indian wars battle site research told the author that he has been able to crawl to within seventy-five feet of where the corral's north wall is believed to have been located without being spotted by an observer at the monument. Comments, Fenn to author, February 4, 1990.

93. Hebard/Brininstool, *The Bozeman Trail*, Vol. II, p. 50.

94. *Ibid.,* p. 53.

95. See sketch of the corral in Hebard/Brininstool, *The Bozeman Trail*, Vol. II, p. 55.

96. Powell, Letter to Adjutant, Ft. Phil Kearny, August 4, 1867.

97. Hebard/Brininstool, *The Bozeman Trail*, Vol. II, pp. 53-54.

98. *Ibid.,* p. 76.

99. Hebard/Brininstool, *The Bozeman Trail*, Vol. II, pp. 39-87; Powell, Letter to Adjutant, Fort Phil Kearny, August 4, 1867.

100. If the sketch of the corral as found in *The Bozeman Trail* is accurate, it is difficult to imagine how Max Littman could have failed to note a mounted charge. See Hebard/Brininstool, *The Bozeman Trail*, Vol. II, p. 55.

101. *Ibid.,* p. 53; Appleman, "The Wagon Box Fight," pp. 151-152.

102. *Ibid.,* p. l55; Hebard/Brininstool, *The Bozeman Trail,* Vol. 11, pp. 53-54. The 1980 Olympic record for the javelin throw was approximately 100 yards. Considering that this was accomplished by a trained athlete hurling a perfectly balanced spear (lance) under ideal conditions it seems likely that these Indian spears would have to have been launched from a much closer distance in order to reach the corral, assuming that they actually did so. The closest to the corral that a bullet fired from the weapon of a defender has been found is approximately fifty yards, and was apparently fired toward the southeast. Comments, Fenn to author, February 4, 1990. Since the publication of the Third Edition of this book, I discussed the question of spears with Joseph Marshall, himself a Native American and recognized authority on Indian warfare. He explained that the spear was a very personal weapon; that much care went into creating a spear and it was unlikely a warrior would throw one away, which would certainly have been the case at the Wagon Box Fight, since retrieval was impossible. See also Carlson, *The Plains Indians,* p. 61.

103. Powell, Letter to Adjutant, Fort Phil Kearny, August 4, 1867. Stanley Vestal felt that too much emphasis was placed on the Indians reaction to the new breech-loaders. He says they were probably impressed but not overly so. George Bird Grinnell, on the other hand, claimed the Indians were mystified and referred to these weapons as "Medicine Guns" See Vestal, *Warpath,* p. 82; Grinnell, "The Wagon Box Fight," p.4. Based on his discussions with Indian friends, Luther North claimed that after one volley of fire from the corral, the Indians withdrew and that the remainder of the fight consisted mainly of sniping. See North to Reckmeyer, 2 Marc, 1927. Powell was likely referring to the hill east of the present stone marker, which is about 700-750 yards from the corral site. This hill may well have served as the Indians' command post, to the extent that such a term fits their conduct of a battle. If Red Cloud was indeed present this is probably where he would have stationed himself. Comments, H. Sterling Fenn to author, February 4, 1990.

104. L. C. Bishop who was actively involved in historic site research for the Wyoming Historical Society in the 1950s believed the Indians had 28-30 Spencer carbines from the Fetterman fight. See Bishop to Gordon Pouliot, September 21, 1959.

105. Murphy to Hebard, February 15, 1929; Hebard/Brininstool, *The Bozeman Trail,* Vol. II, pp. 54,58,79.

106. A typical Civil War forage cap will hold about 120 rounds of .50-70-450 ammunition. Comments, Fenn to author, February 4, 1990; Hebard/Brininstool, *The Bozeman Trail,* Vol. II, pp. 57-59, 81.

107. Powell, Letter to Adjutant, Fort Phil Kearny, August 4, 1867. In the previous edition, I suggested that these spectators were non-combatants. However, based on a re-reading of Powell's report, I have since concluded that these "spectators" were probably part of the war party, though some non-combatants may have been present, too.

108. *Ibid.,* pp. 57-58; Letter, Gibson to Pitman, February 19, 1924.

109. Hebard/Brininstool, *The Bozeman Trail*, Vol. II, pp. 58-60.

110. Hebard/Brininstool, *The Bozeman Trail*, Vol. II, pp. 62-63. For Baker's story, see *The Denver Post*, August 1, 1919.

111. Gibson to Pitman, March 23, 1925. According to Littman, Jenness was killed about ten minutes after Powell returned from Little Piney Creek. See Camp Notes on the Wagon Box Fight, Hagan Coll. T. C. Diers claims that Jenness had been brooding over an unmerited reprimand from Powell. See Diers, "The Wagon Box Fight," p. 196.

112. *Ibid.*, February 19, 1924; Hebard/Brininstool, *The Bozeman Trail*, Vol. II, pp. 58, 78, 83-84.

113. Hebard/Brininstool, *The Bozeman Trail*, Vol. II, pp. 76, 79. Gibson says the smoke from the smoldering hay and manure didn't really bother them because there was enough wind from the east to blow it away. Letters, Sam Gibson to Theodore Pitman, February 19, 1924, September 19, 1924. However, Gibson contradicted himself about the effect of the smoke in a description of the fight that appeared in *The Denver Post* on August 1, 1919, in which he said "the smoke became dense and sickening," and Littman said the "terrible stench and smoke nearly strangled us at times." Hebard/Brininstool, *The Bozeman Trail*, Vol. II, p.76. George Bird Grinnell said that Young Little Wolf told him that after one or two attacks, the soldiers set fire to the grass, but no other account mentions this. Grinnell to Luther North, March 14, 1927.

114. Hebard/Brininstool, *The Bozeman Trail*, Vol. II, pp. 63-64.

115. *Ibid.*, pp. 64-65, 77; "An Old Time Indian Fighter," *Cheyenne State Leader*, August 23, 1916; Vestal claimed that this individual was Jipala, a Minniconjou Sioux, but also acknowledges that "Jipala" is not a Sioux name. Sam Gibson said he was a Cheyenne medicine man, but doesn't explain how he knew this. See Vestal, *Warpath*, p. 77; Letter, Gibson to Pitman, January 20, 1924. Also, if he was armed with a lance, plus bow and arrows, what did he do with the former while using the latter?

116. Hebard/Brininstool, *The Bozeman Trail*, Vol. II, p. 81. I assume the wood train did manage to return, but that is speculation on my part. Since Lieut. Francis McCarthy commanded the escort for the wood train that left the corral on the morning of the fight, and then later accompanied Maj. Smith as a member of the relief party, I assume he and the wood train reached the fort safely.

117. Major Benjamin Smith, Letter to Adjutant, Fort Phil Kearny, August 3, 1867.

118. "An Old Time Indian Fighter, *Cheyenne State Leader*, August 23, 1916.

119. It seems most unlikely that a defender would have been able to make such an identification. See *Winners of the West*, September 1938, p. 8.

120. Hebard/Brininstool, *The Bozeman Trail*, Vol. II, pp. 66-67. It is doubtful that any of the defenders would have known Red Cloud's nephew.

121. *Ibid.*, pp. 65-68.

122. *Ibid.*, p. 67. The hill is 700-750 yards and would have been within range.

123. Littman to Camp, August 22, 1919.

124. Major Benjamin Smith, Letter to Adjutant, Fort Phil Kearny, August 3, 1867.

125. Hebard/Brininstool, *The Bozeman Trail*, Vol. II, p. 68; Murphy, "The Forgotten Battalion," p. 395.

126. Smith, Letter to Adjutant, Fort Phil Kearny, August 3, 1867. Smith's count is wrong. Thirteen soldiers had been assigned as wood camp guards: nine with the main party and four at the side camp. Since all four side camp guards were apparently killed, the most that could have come in would be nine. See also Geier, "The Side Camp," p. 16.

127. Hebard/Brinstool, *The Bozeman Trail*, Vol. II, pp. 69-70.

128. Letter, Gibson to Pitman, January 20, 1924; Brady, *Indian Fights and Fighters*, p. 69.

129. The Annual Report of the Secretary of War for 1867 states that the losses amounted to one officer and five enlisted men killed and two enlisted men wounded.

130. Powell, Letter to Adjutant, Fort Phil Kearny, August 4, 1867; Hebard/Brininstool, *The Bozeman Trail*, Vol. II, pp. 57, 66-67, 70, 78; Brady, *Indian Fights And Fghters*, p.68; Neihardt, *Black Elk Speaks*, p. 16. Olson, *Red Cloud and the Sioux: Problem*, pp. 64-65.

131. Grinnell, Hyde, and Vestal, have all advanced convincing arguments refuting the claim of heavy Indian casualties. Willis Rowland, government interpreter at the Lame Deer (Cheyenne) Agency also downplays the notion of heavy Indian casualties, claiming that these did not exceed fifty, which includes three Cheyennes killed and six or seven wounded. See News Release from Richard Randolph, Lame Deer, Montana, April 18, 1927. In support of Rowland, John Hunton, who was employed at the Fort Laramie sutler's store at the time also said that he never heard of more than fifty Indians killed. See Hunton to Reckmeyer, March 23, 1927 and February 15, 1929. See also Vestal, *Warpath*, p. 6; Hyde, *Red Cloud's Folk*, p. 159; Olson, *Red Cloud and the Sioux Problem*, p. 65. See also, the letters to C. Reckmeyer of Fremont, Nebraska, all in possession of Nebraska State Historical Society: from Luther North, March 22 and April 8, 1927; George Bird Grinnell, April 11, 1927; Grace Raymond Hebard, April 9, 16 and 18, 1927. Under the circumstances, Powell's estimate would seem the most reasonable. He was an officer with combat experience, and as such was accustomed to seeing large bodies of troops maneuvering under battlefield conditions. Consequently, he would have been a better judge than most when it came to estimating both casualties and numbers involved. J. R. Porter, boss of the woodcutters agreed with Powell, estimating 50-60 Indians killed and 2-300 wounded. Porter also later claimed that the ground occupied by the Indians was covered with bits of bandages and pools of blood. *Omaha Weekly Republic*, September 4, 1867, and *Omaha Daily Herald*, August 23, 1867. See also Murphy to Hebard, 5 February, 1917.

132. Smith, Letter to Adjutant, Fort Phil Kearny, August 3, 1867.

133. Garber, "The Site of the Wagon Box Fight," p. 18.

134. *Ibid.* Grace Raymond Hebard was very active in various Wyoming historical projects. In addition to her position on the Landmarks Commission, she was Wyoming State Regent of the DAR and secretary of the Wyoming Oregon Trail Commission.

135. *Sheridan* (Wyo) *Press,* June 30, 1916.

136. *Ibid.*

137. "The Wagon Box Fight," Interview with Max Littman, pp. 20-21. Copy from Grace Raymond Hebard Collection, (In 2-bat-wb), American Heritage Center, University of Wyoming, Laramie, Wyoming.

138. Letter, Grace Raymond Hebard to Lieut. J. M. Young, June 22, 1929.

139. *Ibid.*

140. *Ibid.*

141. Garber, "The Site of the Wagon Box Fight;" *Old Travois Trails,* Vol. 11, No. 2, pp. 19-20; Walter Camp to T.C. Diers August 26, 1919; Diers to Camp, August 29, 1919.

142. Hebard, "The Wagon Box Fight," Marking The Oregon Trail, The Bozeman Road and Historic Places in Wyoming, 1908-1920, DAR, p. 43. Hebard to Lieut. J. M. Young, June 22, 1929; Garber, "The Site of the Wagon Box Fight."

143. *Ibid.*

144. Spear, *Bozeman Trail Scrapbook,* p. 31; Murray, *Military Posts,* pp. 96-97.

145. *Sheridan* (Wyo) *Press,* March 21, 1936; J.W. Vaughn, Letter to author, July 6, 1966.

146. *Sheridan* (Wyo) *Press,* May 26, 29, 31, 1936; Bishop to Lola Homsher, June 22, 1959.

147. *Chicago Westerners Brand Book,* Vol. VII, No. 7, September 1950.

148. *Ibid.*

149. Both Walter Camp and Grace Hebard supported the conclusions of the two old soldiers. However, Hebard's argument also carries the weight of archaeological findings. The late J. W. Vaughn, who did much battlefield research with a metal detector was not at all inclined to accept the memory of old veterans and pointed out how, many years later, General Anson Mills had to make three trips to the site of the Slim Buttes battle where he had been in command, before locating the correct site. And General Charles King, who had been in the Fifth Cavalry at the Battle of War Bonnet Creek never was able to find the place. See Vaughn to Bishop, August 4, 1959.

150. Oslund, Carl, "Map of the Wagon Box Fight, August 2, 1867"; Fenn to Author, February 4, 1990; Bishop to Vaughn, August 19, 1959.

151. Hammer, The Springfield Carbine, pp. 1-2; Vaughn to Author, July 6, 1966; Fenn to Author, February 4, 1990; Bishop to Homsher, June 22, 1959; Bishop to Rickey, July 30, 1959. See also the Archaeological Summary in Appendix Two.

Bibliography

Historical Documents Collections

Camp, Walter, Little Bighorn Battlefield National Monument.

Camp, Walter, Field Notes, Envelope 71, Lilly Library, Indiana University, Bloomington, Indiana.

Hagan, Barry J., Wyoming Room, Sheridan County, Fulmer Public Library, Sheridan, Wyoming.

Hebard, Grace Raymond, American Heritage Center, University of Wyoming, Laramie, Wyoming.

Murray, Robert A., Wyoming Room, Sheridan County, Fulmer Public Library, Sheridan, Wyoming.

Government Documents, Official Reports

Fort Phil Kearny, Post Returns, 1866-1868. Microfilm Copy, National Archives.

Hoover, John M., Affidavit regarding location of wagon box corral.

Miller, Mark E., Jeffrey Hauff & Danny N. Walker, eds., *Historical Archaeology At The Wagon Box Battlefield* (48SH129) Sheridan and Johnson Counties, Wyoming. Cheyenne, WY: Office of the Wyoming State Archaeologist, Division of Cultural Resources Division of State Parks and Historic Sites, Wyoming Department of Commerce, January 1997.

Powell, Captain James, Letter to Adjutant, Fort Phil Kearny, August 4, 1867.

Powell, James, "Pension File," Record Group 15, National Archives.

Reiss, David and Skylar S. Scott, "Archaeological and Historical Investigations at the Wagon Box Fight, Sheridan, Wyoming, 1982."

Smith, Major Benjamin F., Letter to Adjutant, Fort Phil Kearny, August 3, 1867.

Twenty-seventh Regiment of Infantry, "Descriptive Books," National Archives, Record Group 393.

Wyoming, State Survey of Historic Site of Wagon Box Fight, Prepared by Claude L. Gettys, March 19, 1959.

Correspondence/Diaries

Bishop, L.C., Copies of Correspondence with: Elsa Spear Byron, Lola Homsher, Gordon Pouliot, Don Rickey Jr, J.W. Vaughn. Found in the Archives of the Wyoming Pioneer Memorial Museum, Douglas, Wyoming.

Camp, Walter, Copies of Correspondence with: T.C. Diers, Gen. E.S. Godfrey, Gen. Charles King, C.H. Laub, Max Littman, W.N. Magill, J.I. Minnich, William Murphy. Found in the Archives of Little Bighorn Battlefield National Monument, and the B.J. Hagan and Robert A. Murray Collections, Sheridan County, Wyoming, Fulmer Public Library.

Fenn, H. Sterling, Correspondence with Author.

Gibson, Samuel, Correspondence with Theodore Pitman. Reproduced in *The Chicago Westerners Brand Book*, Vol. XXIX, July 1972, No. 5.

Gordon, General David S., Correspondence with Bates, General A. E. B. J. Hagan Collection, Sheridan County, Wyoming, Fulmer Public Library.

Hebard, Grace Raymond, Copies of Correspondence with: Earl A. Brininstool, J.G. Masters, William Murphy, Clarence Reckmeyer, Lieutenant J.M. Young. Archives of Hebard Collection, American Heritage Center, University of Wyoming, Laramie, Wyoming.

Reckmeyer, Clarence, Copies of Correspondence with: George Bird Grinnell, Grace R. Hebard, Luther H. North. Archives of Hebard Collection, American Heritage Center, University of Wyoming, Laramie, Wyoming.

Ten Eyck, Captain Tenodor, Diary, 1866-1867. Transcribed from original in Special Collections Department, University of Arizona Library, Tucson by Susan Badger Doyle.

Maps

Oslund, Carl, "Map Showing Location of Monument and Markers set for the Wagon Box Fight of August 2, 1867."

Articles

Author unknown, "Wagon Box Battle Fiercest in West," *The Denver Post*, August 1, 1919.

———, "The Indian Troubles Fort Philip Kearny, August 5, 1867," *Review and Examiner*, Washington, D.C. B.J. Hagan Collection, Sheridan County, Wyoming, Fulmer Public Library.

———, "The Wagon Box Fight," Hebard Collection. American Heritage Center, University of Wyoming, Laramie, Wyoming.

Bate, Walter N., (Compiler), "Eyewitness Accounts of the Wagon Box Fight," *Annals of Wyoming*, Vol.41, No. 2, October 1969.

DeLand, Charles, "The Sioux Wars," South Dakota Historical Collections, Vol. XV, 1930.

Diers, Theodore C., "The Wagon-Box Fight," *Prairie Schooner*, Vol. 7, No. 3, 1928.

Doyle, Susan Badger, "The Bozeman Trail, 1863-1868," *Annals of Wyoming*, Vol. 70, No. 2, Spring 1998.

Garber, Vie Willits, "The Site of the Wagon Box Fight," *Old Travois Trails*, Vol. II, No.2, July-August 1941.

Geier, George, "The Side Camp," *Old Travois Trails*, Vol. II, No. 2, July-August 1941.

Griggs, Burt, Interview with Frederic Claus, "The Truth About the Wagon Box Fight," *Sheridan Post Enterprise*, July 21, 1921.

Grinnell, George Bird, "The Wagon Box Fight," *Midwest Review*, Vol. IX, No's 2 and 3, February-March 1928.

Guthrie, John, "John Guthrie's Account of the Wagon Box Fight," *Winners of the West*, Sept. 1939. (Copy found in Hagan Collection, Sheridan County, Wyoming, Fulmer Public Library).

Hebard, Grace R., "The Wagon Box Fight," *Marking The Oregon Trail, The Bozeman Road and Historic Places in Wyoming, 1908-1920*, The Daughters of the American Revolution, pp. 42-43.

Hilman, Fred W., "The Wagon Box Monument," *Old Travois Trails*, Vol. II, No. 2, July-August 1941.

Hurwitz, Reva, "Man Who Knew Local Area Before Founding of Cheyenne," *Wyoming State Tribune-Cheyenne State Leader*, March 20, 1941.

Keenan, Jerry, "Max Littmann: Immigrant Soldier in the Wagon Box Fight," *Western States Jewish Historical Quarterly*, Vol. VI, No.2, January 1974.

King, S. E., "Officially Locate Famous Battlefield," *The Sheridan Post*, August 3, 1919.

Koster, John, "Wagon Box Fight," *U.S. Army Infantry Magazine*, 1978.

Lemmon, G. E., "The Wagon Box Fight—Big Horn Mountain Country 1867," in Stories of Pioneer Life Assembled 1936-1938, Wyoming Collection, WPA Project. (Copy from Hagan Coll.).

Littman, Max, "An Old Time Indian Fighter Tells Story of Early Days," *Cheyenne State Leader*, August 23, 1916.

Lowe, James A., "The Bridger Trail: An Alternative Route to the Gold Fields of Montana Territory in 1864," *Annals of Wyoming*, Vol. 70, No. 2, Spring 1998.

Mattmueller, Rosella, "The Wagon-Box Corral Fight: Red Cloud's Great Defeat." *Western Horseman*, March 1952.

Murphy, William, "The Forgotten Battalion," *Annals of Wyoming*, Vol. VI & VII, No.2, October 1929.

Reckmeyer, Clarence, "The Truth About The Wagon Box Fight." No publisher. 1927. A collection of comments and quotes found in the Hagan Collection., Sheridan County, Wyoming, Fulmer Public Library.

Reisch, Sonny, "The Wagon Box Fight," *The Sentry*, (Published by the Gatchell Museum Association, Inc.), Vol. 1, No. 3, July 1992.

Richardson, E. M., "The Forgotten Haycutters at Fort C.F. Smith," *Montana: The Magazine of Western History*, Vol. IX, No. 3, July 1959.

Sinclair, F. H., "White Man's Medicine Fight: Wyoming's Dramatic Wagon Box Battle," *Montana: The Magazine of Western History*, Vol. VI, No.3, July 1956.

Schreibeis, Charles D., "The Wagon Box Fight," *Old Travois Trails*, Vol. II, No.2, July-August 1941 (also appears in Vol. III, No.1, May-June 1942).

Shockley, Lt. P.M., "The Wagon Box Fight The Last Important Event of Fort Phil Kearny's Short Existence," *Quartermaster Review*, September-October 1932.

Straight, Michael, "The Strange Testimony of Major Powell," *NY Westerners Brand Book*, Vol. VII, 1960.

Teepee Book, August 1915 July 1916.

True West, Vol. VII, No.5, May-June 1960.

Western Farm Life, Vol. 60, No.13, July 1958.

Books

Appleman, Roy E., "The Wagon Box Fight," in *Great Western Indian Fights*, Garden City, NY: Doubleday & Company, 1960.

Brady, Cyrus Townsend, *Indian Fights and Fighters*, New York: The McClure Co., 1904.

Brown, Dee, *Fort Phil Kearny: An American Saga*, New York: G.P. Putnam's Sons, 1962.

Carlson, Paul H., *The Plains Indians*. College Station, TX: Texas A&M University Press, 1998.

Carrington, Frances C., *My Army Life: A Soldier's Wife at Fort Phil Kearny*. Boulder, CO: Pruett Publishing Co., 1990.(Reissue of *Army Life on the Plains*, Philadelphia, 1910).

Carrington, Margaret Irvin, *Absaraka, Home of the Crows*, Lincoln, NE: University of Nebraska Press, 1983.

David, Robert Beebe, *Finn Burnett, Frontiersman*, Glendale, CA: Arthur H. Clark Co., 1937.

Dodge, Colonel Richard Irving, *33 Years Among Our Wild Indians*, New York: Archer House, 1959.

Dunn, Jacob B., *Massacres of the Mountains*, New York: Archer House.

Forsyth, George A., *The Story of a Soldier*, New York: D. Appleton and Co., 1900.

Fort Phil Kearny/Bozeman Trail Association Members, *Portraits of Fort Phil Kearny*. Banner, WY: The Fort Phil Kearny/Bozeman Trail Association, 1993.

Hammer, Kenneth M., *The Springfield Carbine on the Western Frontier*, Bellevue, Nebraska: Old Army Press, 1970.

Hans, Fred M., *The Great Sioux Nation*, Minneapolis, MN: Ross and Haines, Inc., 1964.

Hebard, Grace Raymond and E.A. Brininstool, *The Bozeman Trail*, Two Volumes. Lincoln, NE: University of Nebraska Press, 1990.

Heitman, Francis B., *Historical Register and Dictionary of the U.S. Army*, Urbana, IL: University of Illinois Press, 1965.

Howard, James H., *The Warrior Who Killed Custer*, Lincoln, NE: University of Nebraska Press, 1969.

Hyde, George E., Red Cloud's Folk, Norman, OK: University of Oklahoma Press, 1967.

Larson Robert W., *Red Cloud Warrior-Statesman of the Lakota Sioux*. Norman, OK: Univ. of Oklahoma Press, 1997.

Lord, Francis A., *The Civil War Collector's Encyclopedia*, Harrisburg, PA: The Stackpole Co., 1963.

Murray, Robert A., *The Army on the Powder River*, Bellevue, NE: Old Army Press, 1969.

——, *Military Posts in the Powder River Country of Wyoming*, 1865-1894, Lincoln, NE: University of Nebraska Press, 1968.

Neihardt, John G., *Black Elk Speaks*, Lincoln, NE: University of Nebraska Press, 1961.

Olson, James C., *Red Cloud and the Sioux Problem*, Lincoln, NE: University of Nebraska Press, 1965.

Piney Island: A Guide to the Story Area, Story, Wyoming, 1970.

Sandoz, Marie, *Crazy Horse*, New York: Hastings House, 1955.

Spear, Elsa, *Bozeman Trail Scrapbook*, Sheridan, WY: The Mills Co., 1967.

——, *Fort Phil Kearny, Dakota Territory, 1866-1868*, Sheridan, WY: 1939.

Vaughn, J.W., *Indian Fights: New Facts on Seven Encounters*, Norman, OK: University of Oklahoma Press, 1966.

Vestal, Stanley, *Warpath*, Boston, MA: Houghton, Mifflin, 1934.

Weigley, Russell F., *History of the United States Army*. New York: Macmillan Publishing Co., Inc., 1967.

Wellman, Paul I., *The Indian Wars of the West*, Garden City: Doubleday & Co., 1956.

References Cited in the Archaeological Report

Barber, John L. *The Rimfire Cartridge in the United States & Canada: an Illustrated History of its Manufacturers and Their Products, 1857-1984.* Armory Publications, Tacoma, Washington, 1987.

Barnes, Frank C. *Cartridges of the World.* Fourth Edition. DBI Books, Inc., Northfield, Illinois, 1980.

Berge, Dale L. *Simpson Springs Station: Historical Archaeology in Western Utah.* Bureau of Land Management, Cultural Resource Series, No. 6, 1980.

Brown, Dee. *The Fetterman Massacre.* Originally published in 1962 as *Fort Phil Kearny: An American Saga* by G. P. Putnam's Sons. University of Nebraska, Lincoln, 1971.

Cavalry School, The. *Horsemanship and Horsemastership.* Volume II, Part Four – Horseshoeing. Originally published in 1935. Academic Division, the Cavalry School, Fort Riley, Kansas, 1988.

Claus, Frederic. "My Experience in the Wagon Box Fight." In *The Bozeman Trail, Volume II,* by Grace Raymond Hebard and E. A. Brininstool, pp. 82-87. Originally published in 1922. University of Nebraska Press, Lincoln, 1991.

Connor, Mellissa, and Douglas D. Scott. *Metal Detector Use in Archaeology: An Introduction. Historical Archaeology* 32(4):76-85, 1998.

Davis, Don P. "From Square One: an Examination of the New Cut Nail Business in America," in *The Wyoming Territorial Prison Archaeology Project: Historical Archaeology of a Frontier Institution,* edited by Charles A. Reher and Marcel Kornfeld, pp. 448-457. Draft report submitted to the Wyoming State Archives, Museums, and Historical Department. On file at the Department of Anthropology, University of Wyoming, Laramie, 1998.

Eckles, David. Continued Archeological Investigations at the Wagon Box Fight, Sheridan County, Wyoming. Report submitted to the Wyoming Recreation Commission. On file at the Office of the Wyoming State Archaeologist, Laramie, 1984.

Ferguson, Leland G. *Archeology at Scott's Lake, Exploratory Research, 1972, 1973.* Research Manuscript Series No. 68. Institute of Archeology and Anthropology, University of South Carolina, Columbia, 1975.

Fox, Richard Allan, Jr. *Archaeology, History, and Custer's Last Battle.* University of Oklahoma Press, Norman, 1993.

Fox, Richard Allan, Jr., and Douglas D. Scott. "The Post-Civil War Battlefield Pattern: an Example from the Custer Battle." *Historical Archaeology* 25(2):92-103, 1991.

Gibson, Samuel S. "The Wagon Box Fight," in *The Bozeman Trail, Volume II,* by Grace Raymond Hebard and E. A. Brininstool, pp. 39-71. Originally published in 1922. University of Nebraska Press, Lincoln, 1990.

Haecker, Charles M., and Jeffrey G. Mauck. *On the Prairie of Palo Alto: Historical Archaeology of the U. S.-Mexican War Battlefield.* Texas A&M University Press, College Station, 1997.

Hamilton, T. M. *Native American Bows.* Missouri Archaeological Society Special Publications No. 5, Columbia, Missouri, 1982.

Hanson, James. Upper Missouri Arrow Points. *The Museum of the Fur Trade Quarterly* 8(4):2-8, 1992.

Hatcher, Julian S. *Firearms Investigation, Identification, and Evidence.* The Stackpole Company, Harrisburg, Pennsylvania, 1957.

Haven, Charles T., and Frank A. Belden. *A History of the Colt Revolver and Other Arms Made by Colt's Patent Fire Arms Manufacturing Company from 1836-1940.* Bonanza Books, New York, 1940.

Hebard, Grace Raymond, and E. A. Brininstool. *The Bozeman Trail.* Two Volumes. Originally published in 1922. University of Nebraska Press, Lincoln, 1990.

Hilman, Fred W. The Wagon Box Monument. *Old Travois Trails* 2(2):22, 1941.

Horn, Houston. *The Old West: The Pioneers.* Time-Life Books, New York, 1974.

Hume, Ivor Noel. *Historical Archaeology.* Alfred A. Knopf, New York. (Fifth Printing 1980), 1968.

Keenan, Jerry. *The Wagon Box Fight.* Third Edition. Lightning Tree Press, Boulder, Colorado, 1992.

Lewis, Berkeley. *Small Arms Ammunition at the International Exposition, Philadelphia, 1876.* Smithsonian Studies in History and Technology 11, 1972.

Limerick, Patricia Nelson. *The Legacy of Conquest: the Unbroken Past of the American West.* W. W. Norton & Company, New York, 1987.

Haunted America. In *Sweet Medicine: Sites of Indian Massacres, Battlefields, and Treaties*, photographs by Drex Brooks, pp. 119-163. University of new Mexico Press, Albuquerque, 1995.

Logan, Hershel C. *Cartridges: a Pictorial Digest of Small Arms Ammunition.* Bonanza Books, New York, 1959.

MacAdam, Walter K. *Beyond the Bozeman Trail: the Story of Captain Alexander Wishart.* Westways Publishing, New Hampshire, 1996.

Marcot, Roy M. *Spencer Repeating Firearms.* Northwood Heritage Press, Irvine, California, 1983.

Marshall, S. L. A. *Crimsoned Prairie: the Indian Wars.* Da Capo Press, Inc., New York, 1972.

McChristian, Douglas C. *The U. S. Army in the West, 1870-1880: Uniforms, Weapons, and Equipment.* University of Oklahoma Press, Norman, 1995.

McGonagle, Roberta Lee. Metal Projectile Points from the Deapolis Site, North Dakota. *Plains Anthropologist* 18:218-227, 1973.

Miller, Mark E., and Dale L. Wedel. *Archaeological Survey and Test Excavations at Fort Fred Steele State Historic Site.* Report submitted to Wyoming

Department of Commerce. On file at the Office of the Wyoming State Archaeologist, Laramie, Wyoming, 1992.

Miller, Mark E., Jeffrey Hauff, and Danny N. Walker. *Historical Archaeology at the Wagon Box Battlefield (48SH129), Sheridan and Johnson Counties, Wyoming.* Fort Phil Kearny/Bozeman Trail Association, Sheridan, Wyoming, 1997.

Mishkin, Bernard. *Rank and Warfare Among the Plains Indians.* University of Nebraska Press, Lincoln. First Bison Book printing 1992.

Reher, Charles A., and George C. Frison. *The Vore Site, 48CK302, A Stratified Buffalo Jump in the Wyoming Black Hills.* Plains Anthropologist Memoir 16, 1980.

Reiss, David, and Skylar S. Scott. *Archaeological and Historical Investigations at the Wagon Box Fight, Sheridan County, Wyoming.* Report submitted to the Wyoming Recreation Commission. On file at the Office of the Wyoming State Archaeologist, Laramie, Wyoming, 1983.

Archaeological and Historical Investigations at the Wagon Box Fight, Sheridan County, Wyoming. *The Wyoming Archaeologist* 27(3-4):57-78, 1984.

Scott, Douglas D., and Richard A. Fox, Jr. *Archaeological Insights into the Custer Battle: an Assessment of the 1984 Field Season.* University of Oklahoma Press, Norma, 1987.

Scott, Douglas D., Richard A. Fox, Jr., Melissa A. Connor, and Dick Harmon. *Archaeological Perspectives on the Battle of the Little Bighorn.* University of Oklahoma Press, Norman, 1989.

Secoy, Frank Raymond. *Changing Military Patterns of the Great Plains.* First Bison Book printing, University of Nebraska Press, Lincoln, 1992.

Sinclair, F. H. White Man's Medicine Fight. *Montana: The Magazine of Western History* 6(3):1-10, 1956.

Smith, Steven D. Book Review of: Archaeology, History, and Custer's Last Battle, by Richard Allan Fox, Jr. *Historical Archaeology* 29(2):121-122, 1995.

South, Stanley. *Method and Theory in Historical Archeology.* Academic Press, New York, 1977.

Spear, Elsa. *Bozeman Trail Scrapbook: the Books and Photos of Elsa Spear.* Fourth Printing. Published by the Family of Elsa Spear Byron, 1993.

Spivey, Towana (editor). *A Historical Guide to Wagon Hardware & Blacksmith Supplies.* Contributions, Museum of the Great Plains 9, 1979.

Steffan, Randy. *The Horse Soldier 1776-1943, Volume II: the Frontier, the Mexican War, the Civil War, the Indian Wars 1851-1880.* University of Oklahoma Press, Norman, 1978.

Suydam, Charles R. *The American Cartridge: an Illustrated Study of the Rimfire Cartridge in the United States.* G. Robert Lawrence, Santa Ana Gunroom, Santa Ana, California, 1960.

U. S. Cartridges and Their Handguns, 1795-1975. Second Printing. Beinfeld Publishing, Inc., North Hollywood, California, 1979.

Vaughn, J. W. Letter to Gene Galloway, October 23, 1967. Vertical file "Indians—Hostilities—Wagon Box Fight;" Wyoming State Archives, Cheyenne, 1967.

Wallace, Anthony F. C. Psychological Preparations for War. In *War: the Anthropology of Armed Conflict and Aggression*, edited by Morton Fried, Marvin Harris, and Robert Murphy, pp. 173-182. The Natural History Press, New York. Doubleday & Company, Inc. Edition, 1968.

The Fort Phil Kearny/Bozeman Trail Association

The Fort Phil Kearny/Bozeman Trail Association was established to preserve, develop and promote the historic sites at Fort Phil Kearny, the Fetterman and Wagon Box fights, and along the Bozeman Trail.

The Association includes members from nearly every state in the nation and eight foreign countries. Interested individuals are invited to join. For more information, contact The Fort Phil Kearny/Bozeman Trail Association, P.O. Box 5013, Sheridan, WY 82801.

INDEX

Printed in the United States
82594LV00004B/1-48/A